JOSIAH BELDEN
1841 California Overland Pioneer:
His Memoir and Early Letters

JOSIAH BELDEN

1841 California Overland Pioneer:

His Memoir and Early Letters

Edited and with an Introduction by
Doyce B. Nunis, Jr.

THE TALISMAN PRESS

Georgetown, California 1962

Contents

for
John Walton Caughey

Introduction

by Doyce B. Nunis, Jr.

I<small>N</small> 1878, Josiah Belden dictated his memoirs to one of Hubert Howe Bancroft's assistants. The finished manuscript, "Statement of Historical Facts of California by Josiah Belden of Santa Clara Co.," is one of the few documentary sources which relates the rigors of the first planned overland emigration in 1841. Utilizing the central route to the Pacific coast, in 1841, the Bartleson party, of which Belden was a member, blazed a trail that subsequently became the American highway to Eldorado.

Prior to 1841, others had made the overland journey to the shores of the Pacific. The first northern route emigration across the plains was undertaken by Jason and Daniel Lee's small missionary party in 1834, and in 1836, the Whitman-Spalding party. Their destination was Oregon. In the wake of these two missionary bands, in 1840 a fragment of the "Peoria" party arrived, followed by the "Great Reenforcement." From Santa Fé, a number of trading and trapper expeditions ventured to California via the southern route. And a few of the men who made that journey became permanent residents.

The trail taken by the Bartleson company was somewhat similar to that etched by two previous trapper expeditions. Jedediah S. Smith had made the trip in 1826 and

1827, and Joseph R. Walker, employed by Captain Bonneville, in 1833. However, the Bartleson party was unique. As John W. Caughey sees it, the party's significance lies in the fact that it "was the entering wedge for the new type of migration to California": determined emigrants bent on permanent settlement.[1]

Captivated by excited reports on the wonders and opportunities of Mexican California, in late winter of 1840, the Western Emigration Society was established in frontier Missouri. Chief propagandist in urging Americans to head for the "land of perennial spring and boundless fertility" was Antoine Robidoux, a long-time trapper and trader in the transmontane west. "His description of the country made it seem like a paradise," wrote John Bidwell, a charter member of the newly formed society.[2] Robidoux's vivid portrait was soon seconded by Dr. John Marsh, a California resident, in letters to Missouri friends written from the foot of Mt. Diablo. Joseph B. Chiles, who joined the emigrant train, recalled that William Baldridge, a fellow party member, "had been corresponding with Dr. Marsh whose descriptive letters of Cal[ifornia] and its climate and resources, had awakened in him a great desire to see the country . . . ."[3] All of this information found printed exposition in the Missouri press. Within a month, some 500 pledges to undertake the trek west were received by the society.

One St. Louis newspaper, reporting early in 1841 on a subsequent meeting of 58 Jackson County residents gathered to make plans for the western journey, heralded the advantages and challenge awaiting the bold and adventuresome—

The climate is salubrious and delightful—the soil rich—the natural productions various—and all the means of a pleasant and comfortable subsistence afforded in abundance. A glorious era is, no doubt, dawning in those regions so favored by nature; and they who first take possession have all before them to choose. To the young, the buoyant, and the enterprizing the field is full of promise. They may not only grow rich by skill, industry and perseverance; but may achieve the splendid fame of laying deep and broad the foundation of an empire.[4]

But popular enthusiasm soon waned. Thomas J. Farnham, a member of the "Peoria Party" that ventured overland in 1839 to Oregon, returned from the trip disillusioned. His account of his adventures, *Travels in the Great Western Prairies*, was published in 1841, preceded by a disparaging letter that was dutifully, if not gleefully, published in Missouri newspapers. John Bidwell later wrote: "Just at this time [1841], and it overthrew our project completely—was published the letters of Farnham in the New York papers and republished in all the papers of the frontier at the instigation of the Weston [Missouri] merchants and others."[5] In calculating terms the press cautioned: ". . . fellow citizens, if you really wish to lead a quiet, industrious, useful life, if you wish to help on the country to which you owe your birth . . . stay at home."[6] The resolution of the pledged members in the newly-formed emigrant society wilted in the face of Farnham's bleak report and the harsh admonition of the press. But John Bidwell remained firm.

When the appointed May rendezvous at Sapling Grove was at hand, less than a tenth of the original pledged number appeared.[7] Josiah Belden was among those who enrolled in the daring enterprise.

Born in Upper Middletown, Connecticut, May 4, 1815, Josiah Belden could claim direct descent from one of the state's oldest families. In 1645, his English ancestors, Richard and Josiah Bayldon [Belden], settled in Wethersfield, sinking roots into colonial Connecticut's virgin soil.

Early life for Josiah Belden was less than happy; it was plagued with personal tragedy. When he was four years old, his mother, Abigail McKee, died, and when he was fifteen, his father's death forced him to quit school and to seek his subsistence.

An orphan, he moved to Albany, New York, to live with an uncle. After brief residence there, he went to New York City, finding employment as a dry goods store clerk. A few months later, he returned to Albany, apprenticing himself to Luke F. Newland, a jeweler. In place of formal education, Belden sought the security of a trade.

Infected by a desire for travel, on May 4, 1836, he journeyed to New York, then Philadelphia. From there he took passage to Mobile, voyaging on to Liverpool, England; subsequently returning to Philadelphia. Still restless, he "went south to New Orleans" to winter. Moving from there in early 1837, he established himself in mercantile business at Vicksburg, Mississippi; the next year he transferred his commercial activities to Yazoo City. In joint partnership with a Mr. Watton, he opened a general store and cotton exchange emporium.

Dissatisfied with the small returns that came to that endeavor, he sold out to his partner in 1841 and headed up river to St. Louis. Shortly after his arrival, he met up with two enthusiasts who had caught the California fever, Henry L. Brolaski and David W. Chandler; later they were joined by a fourth, George Shotwell. With them, he formed a "mess" for the projected overland trip. After outfitting themselves with the necessary supplies and equipment, the four made for the appointed rendezvous at Sapling Grove.[8]

Because of the lack of response to previous advertisements, the formation of the emigrant company was not undertaken until May 18 near the banks of the Kansas River. There in executive session, the earnest emigrants elected Talbot H. Green, President, and John Bidwell, Secretary. After they adopted rules and regulations for the trail, John Bartleson was elected Captain.[9]

John Bidwell relates that the situation was, to say the least, dire.

> When we reached Sapling Grove, the place of rendezvous, in May, 1841, there was but one wagon ahead of us. For the next few days one or two wagons would come each day, and among the recruits were three families from Arkansas. We organized by electing as captain of the company a man named Bartleson from Jackson County, Missouri. He was not the best man for the position, but we were given to understand that if he was not elected he would not go; and he had seven or eight men with him, and we did not want the party diminished, so he was chosen.[10]

All of the emigrants were green recruits. As for the path westward, Bidwell remarked, "Our ignorance of the route was complete. We knew that California lay west, and that was the extent of our knowledge."[11]

Fortunately for the expedition, news was received that a party of Jesuit missionaries was approaching under the guidance of Thomas Fitzpatrick, an experienced trapper who knew the proper route west to the Rockies. Happily, the California bound emigrants associated themselves under his leadership for a goodly portion of the trip west. When the two groups split, one heading north, the other southwest, Father De Smet commented: "They who had started purely with the design of seeking their fortune in California, and [who] were pursuing their enterprise with the constancy which is characteristic of Americans," broke away at Soda Springs.[12]

After parting company with the missionaries and their guide on August 11, the Bartleson party struck out toward the southwest. [13] Reputedly ignorant of the proper route, the company was not without some knowledge of the trail which lay ahead of them as various party members testify. Belden in his narrative even admits this. Certainly some information was supplied the party by Thomas Fitzpatrick who led the Jesuit band to Soda Springs. Although he had never undertaken the California journey, Fitzpatrick was intimately acquainted with Jedediah Smith and Joseph Walker, companion *mountain men*, who had previously made the trip.[14]

Antoine Robidoux, one of the chief inspirations for the formation of the party, undoubtedly supplied what information he had from his years of traversing the transmontane west. In 1837, accompanied by his brother, Louis, he had made the overland journey to California from Santa Fé, and like Fitzpatrick, had an acquaintance with trappers who had been with Smith and Walker on their travels.[15]

The exploits of the *mountain men* were not unknown to the company. Under date of July 5, while the company was at Independence Rock, Bidwell observed in his journal that the place was named by Captain William Sublette who had once celebrated the 4th there. In a later recollection, Bidwell refers to William Sublette's taking the first wagon train across to South Pass in 1830. Jedediah Smith had been a long-time associate of Sublette prior to 1830, and as a partner in the firm of Smith, Jackson and Sublette had undertaken his two California trips in 1826 and 1827. The activities of that fur firm were reported in detail in various newspaper accounts and in official reports to the government.[16]

Father De Smet in one of his letters mentions Bonneville's 1833 expedition in the transmontane region. Nicholas Dawson later echoed this by referring to "Joel Walker's" California trip, a trip undertaken while he was in the employ of Bonneville. Washington Irving popularized that venture in a book published in 1837.[17]

A map in the possession of Elam Brown, a Missouri friend of John Bidwell's, cast some light on the terrain even though it was inaccurate. Bidwell records, under entry of September 29 in his *Journal* (p. 22): "Traveled about 20 miles, course of the stream was W.N.W. According to the map Mary's river ran WSW. Strong doubts were entertained about this being Mary's river." Nicholas Dawson subsequently observed that the Bartleson party "had some old maps." The maps, however, only proved to be illusory.[18]

By far the best information for the company came from the letters of Dr. John Marsh. Among Marsh's correspondents was Michael Nye, one of the party's members. In a letter to Nye which was published in the local Missouri press, Marsh described a plausible route west from Missouri, urging the recipient "to follow it over the Rockies and Sierras to California, and to come direct to his rancho," situated at the foot of Mt. Diablo. Joseph B. Chiles recalled that the company "had learned through Dr. Marsh's letters the latitude of San Francisco Bay, and they thought the sun sufficient to guide them." Furthermore, among the resolutions adopted by the February meeting of prospective emigrants, one read: "That Marsh's route is believed to be the best by which to cross the mountains."[19] That suggested route compares favorably with the one taken by the emigrant train from Soda Springs.

Bidwell in his *Journal,* under date of October 11, 1841, refers to "Marsh's letter" as helping the company identify what they felt was the "St. Joaquin" River. Eight days later, he commented that Captain Walker had been lost in the Sierra, the region the party was then traveling through, for 22 days.[20] Joseph Chiles in his later recollections also makes mention of Marsh's letters both as an inspiration and as a guide west to California. It would appear that Chiles was also acquainted with the family of George C. Yount in the East, as was Charles Hopper, for in 1841 he brought news to that early California trapper-emigrant from his two daughters. Perhaps he may have seen some of Yount's letters to his children.[21]

A fresh, first-hand account of the trail west to California came to the Bartleson party by sheer coincidence. While on the Green River, still being guided by Fitzpatrick, the caravan met Henry Fraeb on July 23. The meeting was opportune. Fraeb was returning from California, having accompanied Joseph R. Walker there to procure horses. That expedition had arrived in February and departed sometime after April, 1841, for the return journey. Father De Smet wrote on this occasion: "We rested two days upon its [the Green River's] banks with the company of Captain F[raeb], who had just returned from California. What they told us concerning that distant country dissipated many illusions, and caused some of our companion, who traveled for amusement, to return." Fraeb's only warning was that wagons would never be able to make it across the mountains, a prophecy which proved all too true.[22]

Using these various sources of information, coupled with their firm determination and courage, the company safely arrived at Dr. Marsh's rancho at the foot of Mt. Diablo,

November 4, not by chance, but design. The hardships and harrowing experiences of their journey from Soda Springs are described by Belden in his "Statement" and in an 1842 letter to his sister written from Monterey.

Belden's early days in Mexican California are chronicled in his memoir and letters. Suffice it to say that soon after his arrival, he found employment with Thomas O. Larkin, opening a branch store for him in Santa Cruz. A year later, Belden returned to Monterey and clerked for his employer. Several years later they would become partners in developing mutual real estate holdings in San Francisco.[23]

In the spring of 1844, Belden formed a partnership with William G. Chard. They operated a small shop and boarding house for distressed American seamen who threw themselves on the mercy of Thomas O. Larkin, by then United States Consul in Monterey. Profits were modest, but helpful.[24]

The next year Belden became a citizen of the Republic of Mexico.[25] In consequence of his support of Governor Manuel Micheltorena, he was able to procure a grant of 21,000 acres in the upper Sacramento River valley near present-day Red Bluff. Dissolving his partnership, he spent the winter of 1845-1846 with his former trail companion, Robert H. Thomes, and possibly his partner, Chard, in the vicinity of his newly acquired domain.

Returning in early spring 1846, Belden found a position with Captain John Paty in Yerba Buena as his commercial agent. Arriving on horseback in that pueblo on Good Friday, he was immediately arrested by the Alcalde, Don Jesús Noe, for violating the solemnity of the season. He was fined $20.00. William D. M. Howard intervened in his behalf, and the fine was remitted.

In the fall of that year, when Captain Paty closed out his major business affairs in the San Francisco Bay area, Belden was hired by William Heath Davis. In that employment, he journeyed south on firm business to Los Angeles and San Diego. Out of that travel came an appointment as the business partner for Mellus & Howard in San José: thus J. Belden & Co. was established.[26]

Broadening his commercial activities, Belden entered into a partnership with Thomas O. Larkin in the early fall of 1847. By Christmas he became a partner in the exploitation of a quicksilver mine on the rancho of Grove Cook near San José, practically on the eve of James W. Marshall's gold strike on the American River.[27]

After a brief sojourn in the gold fields in 1848, a wiser Belden returned to San José to exploit a more profitable and enduring endeavor as a merchant supplying the needs of the gold-seekers. That, coupled with judicious investments in real estate, built his fortune.

In 1850, a year after his marriage to Sarah Margaret Jones, a pioneer of the 1846 emigration, he was elected the first mayor of San José. The next year he served a term on the City Council.[28]

Versed in the ways of business, he astutely disposed of his store and invested his money in the exploitation of property. As Bancroft attests, "real estate made Belden a capitalist."[29]

William H. Brewer, a scientist attached to the geological survey of the state during the 1860's, made note of Belden's status. On August 29, 1861, while in San José, he confided to his journal:

> ... I went out of town a mile and visited the residence of a wealthy citizen, Mr. Belden. He and his wife had come here early (1841), poor, had got rich, visited Europe, brought back many works of

art, etc. He lives here very comfortably on his money, has a fine house, pretty grounds, etc. We spent two or more hours most pleasantly in looking over pictures, photographs, etc., which he had brought from Europe. He was absent, but his wife appears a very fine and pleasant woman.[30]

Belden had taken a trip to Europe in 1859. On a more extended excursion, 1872-1873, accompanied by his family, he visited not only the continent, but the Middle East. Prior to these overseas voyages, he and his wife had traveled nine months in the East in 1852, followed by a second three months holiday in 1861.

Two years later, January 3, while on a lecture tour to San José, Brewer stayed in the Belden house as a guest. Writing in his journal he observed:

The changes they [the Beldens] have seen in this state in the twenty years they have been here must seem like romance. Like other pioneers he made money, and unlike most of them he saved a snug little sum of it and now lives in very comfortable circumstances indeed.[31]

Belden, indeed, led the good life. His annual income, around $60,000 a year, afforded him leisure and pleasure. The family home, a splendid estate of ten acres near San José, landscaped with formal gardens and practical orchards, was built in 1855. The estate was blessed "with a splendid kitchen garden [in which grew] every variety of fruits and vegetables one usually finds within the grounds of a refined, opulent gentleman."[32]

Although Belden had "the reputation of being a sharp, Shrewd Yankee," he was looked upon in general as "a solid, well educated man of pleasant address," with "shrewd business instincts," who was "an honor to his country and the State." One newspaper reporter characterized him thusly: "Unassuming in his manner, and unostentatious in dress, he passes along in a reflective mood, and seems to garner up the thoughts of other days . . . happy and contented."[33]

During his early maturity a staunch Whig, he quickly gave his allegiance to the Republican party and the cause of the Union in 1860. In 1876, Belden served as a delegate to the Republican National Convention in Cincinnati, casting his ballot for Rutherford B. Hayes. Perhaps that experience turned his eyes permanently eastward, for in 1881, he moved his family to New York City. He became a member of the Union League Club and a director of the Erie Railroad. And it was there, April 23, 1892, that he died.[34]

However, Belden's place in history rests exclusively on his membership in the 1841 Bartleson overland party and early days in California. His dictated memoir, along with his letters to his sister which are included in this volume, insures that end.

In addition to Belden's "Statement," a number of other documentary materials report variously on the 1841 westward journey. Among these are the dictations of three other party members: John Bidwell (1877 and c. 1891), Joseph B. Chiles (1878), and Charles Hopper (1871), all manuscripts copies found in the riches of the Bancroft Library. Of these, only Hopper's has seen publication. His narrative was partly printed in the Napa *Register,* March 16, and in the Napa County *Reporter,* March 23, 1872.

Bidwell's first account, a journal kept while on the journey west, was published by an unknown printer in either Weston or Liberty, Missouri, by 1844.[35] It was sent east (perhaps in the care of Joseph B. Chiles when he returned to Missouri) while Bidwell was employed by

John A. Sutter as his agent in Bodega. The journal bears the date of March 30, 1842. The Bancroft Library has the only known printed copy, entitled, *A Journey to California, with Observations about the Country, Climate and the Route to this Country . . .,* which has since been twice republished.

Charles C. Royce, *John Bidwell,* first republished the journal in a memorial volume to that early pioneer in 1906, along with several later day recollections. The second publication was in a limited edition by John Henry Nash in 1937. Photostat copies of the original can be found in the University Library, University of California at Los Angeles, Huntington Library, and the Missouri Historical Society. In editing the Belden "Statement," reliance has been placed on the 1937 edition.

In 1877, Bidwell dictated his recollections to S. S. Boynton at the request of H. H. Bancroft. Twelve years later, 1889, he wrote another version which appeared serially in *The Century Illustrated Monthly Magazine.* The Chico *Advertiser* later issued them in a posthumous pamphlet, adding a section from a later version to complete the textual narrative (c. 1914). The Citadel Press republished this same edition as a paperback in 1962.

About 1891, Bidwell prepared another version of his memoirs for Bancroft. In that manuscript, he makes reference to the *Century* articles.

Royce in his memorial volume published yet another recollection by Bidwell, "Early California Reminiscences." This was first published in the magazine, *Out West,* and appeared serially in 1904. Royce also used sections from the *Century* series in rounding out his volume's version, for the preface is the same. He apparently used both article series to compile the memorial reprint.

Milo M. Quaife edited the first two installments of the 1889 Bidwell version, which appeared in the *Century* series, omitting Bidwell's recollections on "Frémont in the Conquest of California." This latter section was included in the Royce and 1948 editions, however. Lindley Bynum prepared the 1948 edition under the title, *In California Before the Gold Rush.*

In summary, Bidwell prepared four different recollections. Although they vary in phraseology, the information presented is substantively the same. The original 1877 dictation, however, as well as the 1891 version, have not been published.

One point should be made in respect to Bidwell's later versions. He probably did not have a copy of his original journal at hand. This explains the few conflicts which appear between his 1842 account, his 1877 Bancroft dictation, and the 1889 recollections. His later memory proves surprisingly accurate, however.

Robert H. Thomes' memoir of the trip west, dictated to Albert G. Toomes, was published in the San Francisco *Evening Bulletin,* July 27, 1868, and reprinted in Oscar T. Shuck, (comp.), *California Scrap-Book . . .,* pp. 181-184. Mrs. Benjamin (Nancy A.) Kelsey, the only woman who accompanied the Bartleson party into California, gave her recollections in an interview published in the San Francisco *Examiner,* February 5, 1893; later reprinted by *The Grizzly Bear Magazine* in 1915, and in Minnie B. Heath's 1937 article on Mrs. Kelsey, in the same magazine.

Another member of the Bartleson company wrote his memoirs and published them in 1901, probably in Austin, Texas. This work was republished in 1933 under the title, *Narrative of Nicholas "Cheyenne" Dawson.* It should be noted that Dawson wrote his dated recollections after reading Bidwell's *Century Magazine* articles. Dawson also read Mrs. Kelsey's newspaper interview. Later, he entered into correspondence with Bidwell, discussing events of their 1841 journey prior to penning his own version. Perhaps this is why his narrative of events on the march west is so skimpy in detail.[36]

The Bancroft Library has recently acquired additional Dawson manuscripts. Among the items so far deposited with the library is one of significance for the overland trip: Dawson kept a list of encampments and supposed distances traveled by the California bound party.

Another account of the 1841 venture is found in the diaries of James John. The first portion of the diary, which abruptly ends under entry of August 20, is housed in the Oregon Historical Society. George H. Himes prepared it for publication under the title, "The Diary of James St. Johns," which was printed in the St. Johns [Oregon] *Review* in several installments during the spring of 1906. The remaining portion of the diary is housed in the collections of the Rosenbach Foundation, Philadelphia, Pennsylvania. That copy is a curious item. The Philadelphia manuscript is a condensed version of the Oregon Historical Society diary. My good friend, Dale L. Morgan of the Bancroft Library, who has been of enormous help in searching out this item, writes, under cover of a letter, January 17, 1961: "I suppose it [the Philadelphia manuscript] is a condensation of the original diary the rest of the way to California too, but there is no way of telling. Down to September 5, [1841], the Philadelphia MS. is in a different hand; from September 6 to the arrival at Sutter's, it is in John's own hand. Appended to this diary are 'Extracts from Bidwells journal from the 20th of Oct. to the 5th of Nov.,' covering the period after John separated from the company in the Sierra. These extracts are considerably more terse than the published Bidwell diary, and perhaps closer to the original." Fortunately, Mr. Morgan anticipates publication of this virgin and important manuscript. (Hereafter cited *John Diary.*)

James P. Springer, who went back to Missouri in 1842, but returned to settle permanently in 1852, also kept a diary. It seems that he made several round trips from Missouri to California prior to his last move. After locating himself at Saratoga, about ten miles from San José, he served a term in the legislature, 1859, and died, June 4, 1861, being survived by a wife and daughter. During his several trips, he wrote a number of articles and pamphlets extolling the virtues of California. His diary, however, has yet to come to light. If found, it should prove to be of intrinsic worth, for writing in 1856, he listed with amazing accuracy that portion of the Bartleson company that came to California.[37]

The Reverend Joseph Williams, a trail companion to Soda Springs, Idaho, published his travel account in Cincinnati, 1843. This is now available in the 1955 edited version by LeRoy R. Hafen and Ann W. Hafen, under title, *To the Rockies and Oregon, 1830-1842.*

The last extant documentary material relating to the Bartleson 1841 overland party is found in the writings of the three Jesuit priests who accompanied them to Soda Springs. Father Nicholas Point described his missionary travels in a number of letters, a portion of which touch on the months of May through August when the California-bound emigrants were associated with his missionary band. Those manuscripts are housed in the Collège Sainte-Marie, Montrèal, Canada.[38] He also sketched contemporary scenes of his travels west, several of which portrayed events on the route west to Soda Springs. A number of those sketches are housed in the Jesuit Archives of the Missouri Province, Saint Louis University.[39]

Father Gregory Mengarini's accounts are rather dispersed. A number of his early letters detailing his impression of the West have been published in the *Woodstock Letters*.[40]

Another portion of his letters are housed in the National Library, Rome, Italy. As to whether or not those manuscripts reveal any additional information pertinent to the Bartleson party, I am uninformed. The Jesuit Archives at Saint Louis University also contain a few additional letters that touch on the year 1841. Lastly, in 1884 while serving on the faculty of Santa Clara College, California, Father Mengarini dictated his recollections at the request of several Jesuit friends. A few copies of that narrative were printed as a memorial for private circulation after his death. Albert J. Partoll has edited that dictation, "Mengarini's Narrative of the Rockies," published in *Frontier and Midland* in 1938, and as a separate reprint in *Sources of Northwest History*.

Father De Smet, leader of the Jesuit missionaries, wrote rather extensively on his 1841 experiences. His writings dealing with that fruitful period of his life saw publication first in the United States in 1843 under the title: *Letters and Sketches: With A Narrative of a Year's Residence Among the Indian Tribes of the Rocky Mountains*. That work has seen many subsequent republications, the more recent being found in Reuben G. Thwaites, (ed.), *Early Western Travels*. And a number of this pioneer priest's 1841 letters have been published in Hiram M. Chittenden and Alfred D. Richardson, (eds.), *Life, Letters and Travels of Father Pierre-Jean De Smet, S.J., 1801-1872*.

It should be noted, however, that these published sources of Father De Smet's letters and travels are far from complete. It is to be hoped that his large body of writings will soon see definitive publication since there exists a huge quantity of untouched material which is housed in widely diffused Jesuit and Church archival deposits both here in the United States and especially abroad.

Among all of these sources which touch on the Bartleson party, John Bidwell's accounts are, without question, the most extensive and detailed. Second to him, however, stands Josiah Belden's memoir and early letters, along with the James John Diaries.

Although Belden's version of the 1841 trip adds dimension to the established narrative of that event, his dictation warrants attention for a more significant reason. His comments on the social and cultural life of Mexican California are graphic; his attention to political and military affairs, a bit more than casual. Since he was an eye-witness to the transition period between Mexican and American California, 1841-1848, his recollections form a backdrop for our enlarged and enriched comprehension of that decade.

For this reason I have refrained from making extensive changes in editing his memoir: I wanted the "Statement" to retain its "flavor." In instances where there is an error of fact or spelling which might confound the reader, due notice has been taken. Other than paragraphing the text, and transposing one small section of the dictation to a footnote for clarity, the version which follows is as it appears in the original Bancroft manuscript.

Finally, it should be noted that Belden's "Statement" has been previously published. *Touring Topics* presented the dictation in an unedited form in three successive installments beginning in the June, 1930, issue. This is the first time, however, it has appeared as a book in edited form.

For permission to publish Belden's memoir in this edition, I wish to express my appreciation to Dr. George P. Hammond, Director of the Bancroft Library, University of California, Berkeley. For Belden's early letters, I am indebted to Archibald Hanna, Yale University Library, who granted permission to include the three letters found in the *Coe Collection.*

I wish particularly to voice my appreciation to James de T. Abajian, Librarian, California Historical Society, for his helpful research suggestions. Clyde Arbuckle, San José, kindly allowed me to examine additional correspondence from his personal collection of Belden manuscripts and provided me with copies of several photographs for use as illustrations.

Father William L. Davis, S.J., formerly of Gonzaga University, Spokane, Washington, now attached to Canisus House, Evanston, Illinois, graciously offered his detailed knowledge of the rich and untapped Jesuit and Church archival material pertinent to my research effort. Father John F. Bannon, S.J., Saint Louis University, also contributed information of import.

A special note of thanks is due to Dale L. Morgan of the Bancroft Library. He graciously called my attention to several items of importance and generously shared several recent manuscript discoveries with me in order to further the work at hand.

Several good friends added their personal measure to my effort. Edward Yurick, Assistant Professor of History, Ohio Wesleyan University, helped in the laborious task of proofing and checking the transcribed typescript of Belden's dictation during a brief summer holiday in

Los Angeles. Donald J. Schippers gave of his time and talent in executing the trail-map illustration. Mrs. Laurel Allen and Mrs. Joyce Doetkott shared in typing the final draft of the edited manuscript. My good friend and colleague, Mrs. Elizabeth I. Dixon, provided the Index.

Lastly, John and LaRee Caughey gave the completed manuscript a critical and sympathetic reading. Their advice and encouragement proved invaluable.

But for the generosity of these good people and friends, this effort would be greatly lacking. I stand in their debt.

DOYCE B. NUNIS, JR.

UNIVERSITY OF CALIFORNIA

LOS ANGELES

Footnotes to Introduction

1 *California*, p. 213.
2 Bidwell, *Echoes*, pp. 13-14; Bidwell's dictation to S. S. Boynton, 1877, for H. H. Bancroft, pp. 5-6. *MS*, Bancroft Library. (Hereafter cited Bidwell, *Narrative*.)
3 George D. Lyman, *John Marsh, Pioneer*, pp. 237-338; Joseph B. Chiles, 1878, dictation for H. H. Bancroft, "A Visit to California in Early Times," pp. 2-3. *MS*, Bancroft Library. (Hereafter cited Chiles, *Early Times*.)
4 *The Western Atlas, and Saturday Evening Gazette*, March 6, 1841. Dale L. Morgan, [Newspaper Transcripts] *The Mormons and the Far West*, Henry E. Huntington Library, San Marino, California. (Hereafter cited *DLM Trans.*, HEH.)
5 Farnham's book was published at Poughkeepsie, New York, 1841, and has been reprinted in Reuben G. Thwaites, (ed.), *Early Western Travels*, XXVIII-XXIX. Rockwell D. Hunt, *John Bidwell*, pp. 36-37, notes that Farnham's letter was published in the Liberty, Missouri newspaper. Bidwell, *Narrative*, pp. 7-9; *Missouri Argus*, June 26, 1840. *DLM Trans.*, HEH.
6 *The Western Atlas . . .*, May 1, 1841. *Ibid.*

7   As to the number of emigrants who undertook the trip, consult pp. 126-136.

8   The biographical information on Belden is derived from his "Statement"; *Dictionary of American Biography,* II, 145-146 (although there are some discrepencies in that account); Oscar T. Shuck, *Sketches of Leading and Representative Men of San Francisco* . . ., pp. 919-920; Alonzo Phelps, *Contemporary Biography of California's Representative Men,* I, 246; Frederic Hall, *History of San José* . . ., p. 458; San Francisco *Examiner,* June 3, 1869.

9   The company arrived at the Kansas (actually two miles west of the river) on May 16, striking out on the trail, May 19. John Bidwell, *A Journey to California,* p. 2. (Hereafter cited Bidwell, *Journey.*) Green was using an alias. His real name was Paul Geddes. For an explanation, consult Hubert Howe Bancroft, *History of California,* III, 756-766, and John A. Hussey, "New Light Upon Talbot H. Green," *California Historical Society Quarterly* (hereafter cited *CHSQ*), XVIII (1939), 32-63.

10   John Bidwell, *Echoes of the Past About California,* ed. by Milo Quaife, pp. 21-22. (Hereafter cited Bidwell, *Echoes.*)

11   *Ibid.,* pp. 15-16, although this comment must be taken cautiously. The *Daily Missouri Republican,* May 19, 1841, reported the rendezvous at Sapling Grove as of May 10.

12   *Ibid.,* April 20, 1841, reported the projected expedition of Jesuit missionaries under "Father De Smait" [Smet]. Also, Bidwell, *Echoes,* pp. 23-24.

13   *Ibid.,* pp. 39-65, wherein a later description of the trip is given, one that favorably compares with Bidwell's 1841-1842 journal account.

14   Dale L. Morgan, *Jedediah Smith and the Opening of the West,* Chs. 10, 12; for Walker, John C. Ewer, (ed.), *Adventures of Zenas Leonard, Fur Trapper,* pp. 63-132.
     It should be noted that several of the California-bound party went to Fort Hall to gather information and in an attempt to employ a guide. No guide was to be had, but information they obtained later proved helpful. Bidwell, *Journey,* pp. 14, 22.

15   Alexander Taylor, *Scrapbook, No. 7,* p. 10. Bancroft Library; William S. Wallace, *Antoine Robidoux,* for a brief biographical account; and Joseph J. Hill, "Antoine Robidoux . . .," *Colorado*

Magazine, VII (1930), 125-132.

16   Bidwell, *Journey,* pp. 9, 23, 25. For the exploits of Smith, Jackson and Sublette, see Morgan, p. 28 *et seq.*

17   Hiram M. Chittenden and Alfred D. Richardson, (eds.), *Life, Letters and Travels of Father Pierre-Jean De Smet,* I, 300 (hereafter cited *De Smet Letters*); *Narrative of Nicholas "Cheyenne" Dawson* . . ., pp. 14-15 (hereafter cited *Dawson Narrative*).

18   *Ibid.,* p. 16; Bidwell, *Narrative,* p. 24.

19   Chiles, *Early Times,* p. 3; Lyman, p. 237; "California and Oregon," *Colonial Magazine,* V (1841), 229-230, and *Chamber's Journal,* X (August 21, 1841), 245, published a number of the resolutions adopted.

20   P. 25.

21   Chiles, *Early Times,* pp. 2-3; Berkeley *Gazette,* July 21, 1952, in *Biog. & Obits.* [Scrapbooks], VIII, 31, California Historical Society (hereafter cited CHS); Bancroft, VI, 783.

22   LeRoy R. Hafen and Ann W. Hafen, (eds.), *To the Rockies and Oregon,* p. 230 (hereafter cited *Williams Narrative*), *De Smet Letters,* I, 300; *James John Diary,* microcopy, Bancroft Library; Abel Stearns to Juan Bandini, April 5, 1841. *Stearns Papers,* HEH.

23   As late as June 30, 1844, it would appear that Larkin still was using Belden's services as a clerk. By March 31, 1845, he is referred to as a trader; by 1847, a partner. George P. Hammond, (ed.), *The Larkin Papers* (7 vols. to date; Berkeley and Los Angeles, 1951-1960), II, 157, 173, 355; III; 112, 170-171. (Hereafter cited *Larkin Papers.*)

24   *Chard & Belden Business MSS,* Bancroft Library. The first date entered in these papers is April 6, 1844. The terminal date is given as July 7, 1845. Possibly Belden joined Chard as early as 1843, but this is open to question. Their establishment, an adobe, was called the "Cuarto Vientos," the "Four Winds." Monterey *Cypress,* May 25, 1889.

    Chard came to California in 1831 from New York via New Mexico in a party led by William Wolfskill. Eventually he worked his way up the coast from Los Angeles, arriving in the Santa Cruz area in 1837. During the Alvarado affair of 1840 (explained in the text that follows), he was one of the foreign exiles sent to

San Blas, returning in 1841. In 1844 he procured the Las Flores rancho in Tehama County, putting cattle on it in 1845. This may have been the stimulus for Belden to do the same. By 1847 he settled on his ranch lands and died in 1858.

25 [Unpublished] *Larkin Papers*, XX, 34-37, 46-49, 507-508. *MSS*, Bancroft Library; Belden to Reading, May 7, 1844. *Pierson B. Reading Papers*, California State Library (hereafter cited CSL).

26 Belden's partnership arrangement with the firm of Mellus & Howard probably dates from the spring of 1848. Henry Mellus wrote to William D. M. Howard, March 24, urging him to get Belden "a going." *W.D.M. Howard Papers*, CHS. From 1846-1847, Belden worked for Davis. Belden to Davis, November 18, 1846; May 15, November 6, 1847. *William H. Davis Papers*, CSL.

27 Belden to Davis, March 18, 1847. *Ibid.*; Belden to Larkin, October 1, November 8, December 25, 1847. *Larkin Papers*, VII, 3, 56, 103. For details of the mining partnership, see the *Californian*, February 16, 1848.

28 Belden was elected Mayor, April 13, 1850, and after serving a year, became a City Councilman on April 15, 1851. *San José City Archives*, p. 15.

Belden and his bride were married February 1, 1849, by Kimball Hale Dimmick, Alcalde of San José. Marriage Certificate, *Belden Papers*, courtesy of Clyde Arbuckle; *Alta California*, February 8, 1849. Their marriage was blessed by two sons and three daughters.

29 Bancroft, II, 715; Reuben L. Underhill, *From Cowhides to Golden Fleece*, p. 92 *et seq.*

In February, 1861, Belden purchased one of twenty shares ($10,000 each) to become one of the founding subscribers in the California Mutual Marine Insurance Company. "The California Recollections of Caspar T. Hopkins," *CHSQ*, XXVI (1947), 264.

30 Francis P. Farquhar, (ed.), *Up and Down California in 1860-1864. The Journal of William H. Brewer . . .*, p. 175.

31 *Ibid.*, pp. 365-366.

32 Shuck, pp. 928-929. The residence was built at a cost of $25,000. In 1887 it was purchased by Senator Caleb H. Maddox and moved to a site within the city of San José. *Artistic Homes of California*, [n.p.], September 3, 1887. The Belden property of ten

acres was sold to Maddox for $60,000 and became the site for the Hotel Vendome. H[orace] S. Foote, (ed), *Pen Pictures . . .,* p. 647.

33 Sacramento *Daily Democratic State Journal,* October 27, 1855; Luella Dickenson, *Reminiscenses . . .,* p. 107; San Francisco *Call,* April 24, 1892; *Alta California,* March 23, 1866.

34 Phelps, I, 249; New York *Tribune,* April 25, and New York *Sun,* April 26, 1892. Buried in Woodlawn Cemetery, Belden was survived by his two sons: Charles A. Belden, San Francisco, and George F. of Cincinnati; three daughters: Mrs. Luis Emilio, Mrs. Lewis Morris Iddings, and Mrs. George Rutledge Gibson, all of New York. Belden left an estate reckoned at two million dollars. San Francisco *Call,* April 24, June 19, 1892. His wife died in 1904. San Francisco *Chronicle,* December 3, 1904.

35 Henry R. Wagner, *The Plains and the Rockies,* revised by Charles L. Camp, pp. 130-131.

36 Dawson in his preface states he began writing his narrative on March 1, 1894, and finished it sometime after January 1, 1901, as he mentions on page 101. This would seem to indicate that Robert E. Cowan's publication date, c. 1894, is in error.

Few copies of the original edition are known to exist: one in the library of the University of Texas, the University of California at Los Angeles, the Bancroft, Streeter Collection, and one in the California State Library, Sacramento. The latter library entered the book in its accessions in July, 1901. (Letter from Allen R. Ottley, California Section Librarian, to this writer, January 24, 1962.)

37 San Francisco *Chronicle,* June 12, 1856; San José *Tribune,* July 23, 1856; J. P. Munro-Fraser, *History of Santa Clara County . . .,* p. 741.

38 Letter from Rev. Paul Desjardins, S.J., Archivist at the College, to this writer, June 30, 1960. Father Joseph P. Donnelly, S.J., Marquette University, has edited these manuscripts for publication. Letter to this writer, August 17, 1960.

39 John F. McDermott, "De Smet's Illustrator: Father Nicholas Point," *Nebraska History,* XXXIII (1952), 35-40.

40 Citations given in Carlos Sommervogel, (ed.), *Bibliotheque de la Compagnie de Jesus,* V, 946; references to Fr. Point, VI, 921.

JOSIAH BELDEN:
Statement of Historical Facts

Josiah Belden
(*Courtesy of Society of California Pioneers*)

Historical Statement

by Josiah Belden

I CAME FROM MIDDLETOWN, Ct., lived in Albany from the age of 15 till I was 21, and then went south to New Orleans, spent a winter there, and then went to Mississippi, and was engaged in mercantile business in Vicksburg, and then in Manchester.[1] I sold out there, and went to St. Louis, and after being there a short time, in the spring of 1841, I met with two or three young men there, who told me of an expedition that was being got up to go to California. Being rather fond of that kind of adventure, naturally I agreed with those parties to make up a little mess of our own, four or five of us, procure an outfit at St. Louis, and then proceed to the town of Independence, on the western frontier of Missouri, where this expedition was to be organized, and a company formed for the purpose of proceeding to California. This was the inception of the emigration across the plains. This party opened the road, so to speak, was the beginning. In getting up this expedition, those who joined it had heard some reports about California, but very vague, and they knew but little about it or the means of getting there, and started it as an exploring expedition to find their own way out there, and see what the country was. If it proved attractive, some had an idea of settling there, and others joined it more as a matter of adventure, to see something of Indian life, and indulge in hunting on the plains, and all that kind of thing. For my part, when I was younger, I had read Cooper's novels, and about Astor's expedition to the Columbia River, and that rather excited a desire in my mind to see something of a wild country, of buffalo hunting, and to have some adventures among the Indians.[2] That expedition should have the credit of starting the emigration to California. Those who joined it were really pioneers, for there had been no emigration before; there was nothing known of the road, or how to get there.[3] It was something of a perilous undertaking, and it was the beginning of the whole settlement of this country.

We started from Missouri. Mr. Chandler, Mr. Brolasky, Mr. Shotwell and myself formed the mess from St. Louis. We left that place about the first of May, 1841.[4] We bought a wagon in St. Louis, and the princip[le] things we considered necessary for our outfit, harness, provisions, and some things to trade with the Indians on the road. We went up the Missouri in a steamboat to near Independence. When we got there, we found a number of persons collected from different sections of the country. After being there some days, the company was formed and organized, laid in the necessary provisions, procured an outfit of animals &c. We elected a leader for the company by the name of Bartlettson [Bartleson]. We were all armed, of course.[5]

At Independence, the persons who designed going to California made arrangements with a party of missionaries, who were going to the Columbia River, to the Flathead nation, to travel with them as far as they were going in our direction. They had a man named Fitzpatrick as a sort of leader or guide, who had never been across the continent, but had been a hunter and trapper in the neighborhood of the head waters of the Columbia River.[6] The following were the members of our company: Bartlettson [Bartleson] as Leader, Robt. H. Thomes, now of Tehama, ... Bartlett, Jos. Childs, Major [Robert] Rickman, Josiah Belden, Paul Geddes, Ch.[s] Weber of Stockton, Henry Hubert [Huber], John Bidwell of Chico, [Elias] Barnett, [Henry L.] Brolask[i], Ch.[s] Hopper, Grove Cook, Benj. Kelsey, Andrew Kelsey, Mrs.[Nancy A.] Kelsey, [George] Henshaw, James McMahon, [A. Gwin] Patt[o]n, Nelson McMahon, Nich. Dawson, [James] Dawson, [David W.] Chandler, [Ambrose] Walton, [John L.] Schwartz, [Thomas] Jones, Jas. Littlejohn [Johns], Ch.[s] Flugge, [Michael] C. Nye, [James P.] Springer, Pfeiffer [Fifer].[7] There were about the same number of the missionaries, with their servants and guides, making about 60 all together, who started from Independence.[8]

We left about the 10th of May. We had made some rules for our protection against the Indians, setting guard, patrols &c.[9] The company divided into watches for guard, each taking it in turn. There was one woman in our party Mrs. Kelsey; the missionaries had none.[10] We moved along very gradually; a part of the wagons were drawn by oxen, and part by mules.[11] We had riding animals besides. We took as much provision as we could haul and carry, to last us until we should get into the buffalo country, when we expected to supply ourselves by hunting.

We travelled to the Kansas River, and were ferried across, and followed up the Little Blue (I think it was called) to near its headwater, and then struck across the country to the Platte; a prairie country all through there. We followed up the South fork of the Platte, I think, and in fording lost some animals, and we had considerable trouble to get across finally with all our wagons. We reached Ft. Laramie [June 20], and passed on into the Black Hills, and near the Wind River Mountain, and came to Independence Rock on the Sweetwater Creek [July 5], and when we got into buffalo country, we stopped two or three days and killed buffalo, and jerked the meat, and made packs of that to carry us through. Meantime we were travelling through a country pretty badly infested by the Crow and Blackfeet Indians.

One day one of the party had strayed outside into the country, and a party of Indians came upon him, and robbed him of his gun and ammunition, and after detaining him some time, let him go, and he got onto the trail and joined the company.[12] Soon after, we saw a body of Indians coming up full charge in our rear, as though intending to attack us. They came within several hundred yards. The party stopped, and formed a hollow square with our wagons, and prepared to defend ourselves as well as we could. They halted, and Fitzpatrick, the leader of the missionary party, advanced toward them, and made signs for them to send their Chief for a consultation. They did so, and they had a talk, and they agreed that they would not make any attack upon us, but professed a desire to treat with us, and he made an arrangement with them that we should form a camp there, and a portion of them might come in at night while they were camped a distance off, and then they could treat with us if they wished. A few of them came at night, and smoked the pipe of peace, and said they did not want to fight us. We found them, however, to be a war party of the Cheyenne tribe, about 50 or 60 warriors, fine looking, and they said they were looking for the Pawnees. They were fully armed with bows and arrows and tomahawks, and some few guns. They were the finest looking body of men I ever saw for Indians, quite a formidable looking party. We asked if some of their men had not robbed Dawson of his gun and pistol, and demanded that they should be restored, and they brought them back. They traded a little with us for tobacco and beads, and made no demonstrations of hostility; but we kept a pretty strong guard, and everything passed off peaceably, and we separated from them the next morning.[13]

We went on, following the Sweetwater some distance, and crossing the divide of the Rocky Mountains, and passed on and went down on to Green River, stayed there a day or two, and recruited our animals, and fell in there with a company of trappers under command of a man named Frapp [Fraeb]. They had been sent out by the fur companies from St. Louis. That company of trappers, about 30 or 40, after we left them at Green River, and started on our way west, we afterward learned, left a day or two after we did, and soon after encountered a party of Sioux Indians, and fought with them nearly a day, and had four of their men killed. Frapp [Fraeb] himself among the number, I think. It appeared that we had just missed that party of Indians, and if they had met us, they probably would have whipped us, as the party they encountered were old mountain trappers and Indian fighters, and we had had no experience in that line.[14]

We struck Bear River [August 3] some distance below where the town of Evanston [Wyoming] now is, where the coal mines are, and the railroad passes, and followed the river down. It makes a long bend to the north there, and comes down to Salt Lake. We arrived at Soda Springs, on Bear River and there we separated from the company of missionaries, who were going off towards

Snake River or Columbia. There we lost the services of
their guide Fitzpatrick. Several of our party who had
started to go with us to California also left us there, having
decided to go with the missionaries. Fitzpatrick advised us
to give up our expedition and go with them to Ft. Hall,
one of the Hudson Bay Stations, as there was no road for
us to follow, nothing was known of the country, and we
had nothing to guide us, and so he advised us to give up
the California project. He thought it was doubtful if we
ever got there; we might get caught in the snow of the
mountains and perish there, and he considered it very
hazardous to attempt it. Some four or five of our party
withdrew, and went with the missionaries.[15] About thirty-
one of us adhered to our original intention, and declined
to give up our expedition. As we had attempted to go
to California, we determined we would not give it up, but
continue the attempt, and do the best we could to get
through.[16]

After separating from the missionaries, we followed
Bear River down nearly to where it enters Salt Lake,
about where Corinnes [Corinne, Utah] is now. We had
some knowledge of the Lake from some of the trappers
who had been there. We turned off more to the west and
went round the northerly end of Salt Lake. There we
found a great difficulty in getting water for several days,
all the water near the lake being brackish. We had to make
it into strong coffee to drink it. We went on, hunting our
way along the best we could, amongst the rocks and gullies,
and through the sage brush, working along slowly for a
number of days, aiming to travel westward as fast as we
could, having no other guide than an intention to get west.
After travelling several days, passing over a very desert
country where there was scarcely any food for our animals,

and very rough getting along with our wagons, we finally came to a spot where there was moist ground, some springs, and a little patch of green grass, which we denominated the oasis. We camped there for about a week to recruit our animals. While there we did not know which direction to take, nor how to go, but we had heard before leaving Missouri that there was a river somewhere in that section of the country, which was then called Mary's River, which ran to the westward, and this we thought might be a guide for us in some measure, if we could strike the headwaters of it and follow it west. So while the company were camping there, three of the party who had the best animals started out in a westerly direction, to explore by themselves, and see if they could find any such river, any water running west. After waiting there several days, these men came back, and reported that they had found a small stream of water that seemed to be running westward, and they thought that might perhaps be the headwaters or some branch of the Mary's River that we wished to find.[17] After they returned, we raised camp, and under their direction, as near as we could follow it, we travelled two or three days, I think, and struck this little stream they had spoken of. We followed it down, and found it tended westward, though varying its course, and it proved to be the South fork of Mary's River. We followed it all the way down to the sink of it. Before we struck this river, we found we were so delayed by our wagons that we concluded to abandon them, and we took what things we could and packed them on to our horses and oxen, and what we could not carry, we left with our wagons standing in the plains.

We were then within sight of the Sierra Nevada mountains, which we knew we had to cross. But we could see

no appearance of any opening or depression which we
might avail of to get across. Then we struck south, until
we finally came to what is known as Walker's River. We
then followed the west branch of this river, I think, up
into the mountains. When we struck that river, however,
after following it for some distance and getting into the
neighborhood of the mountains, without finding any depression, or any place where it seemed possible to cross,
there was some division of opinion among the members
of the company. Our provisions had given out before,
while we were travelling down Mary's River, and then we
commenced killing the cattle we had with us and eating
them. At the sink of the Humboldt River, a portion of
the company who had the best animals, about nine of them,
parted from the others, and said they were going to
travel faster, and get in before they became exhausted.[18]
The balance went on, and, as I said, got to Walker's River.
When we reached there, there was a difference of opinion
about whether we should attempt crossing the mountains,
or give up the expedition then, and turn back, and try to
get back to Ft. Hall. While we were stopping there, one
day two others and myself left the party, and went up to
some of the higher peaks of the mountains to explore and
see if we could find any place where we could cross.[19] We
returned and reported that we could see no opening in the
mountains, that so far as we could see, the mountains
seemed to be rather higher beyond than lower, and there
was no appearance of any end or termination of them,
and very little chance to get through. There was a vote
taken in the company to determine whether we should go
on and try to get across the mountains, or turn back and
try to reach Ft. Hall. I think we had only one majority
for going ahead. Although it looked discouraging on the

mountains, my idea was that we should perish in trying to get back to Ft. Hall, and we had better take our chances of getting across the mountains. So we decided to travel on.

The next morning we were packing up to start into the mountains, and in looking back we saw the dust rising on the trail we had travelled the day before, and we waited to see what it was, and presently we saw the nine men who had left us several days before with the idea of going ahead, coming up on our trail, very hungry and forlorn looking. We had a quarter of beef left from the last animal we had killed, and gave them something to eat. They had made a kind of circle, and reached our camp, having struck our trail. We then all went on together.

We worked our way into the mountains with a great deal of difficulty and hardship. The way was very rough, and one day, in winding round the side of a mountain, we lost four of our animals, who missed their footing, and rolled down the mountain. We finally reached the summit with great labor and difficulty, and after getting a little beyond the summit on the other side, we struck a little stream of water that seemed to run westward, and we judged we had got over the divide, and thought that by following the stream as well as we could, it would lead us down the westerly slope of the mountain.

Meantime we had eaten the last of our beef from our cattle, and we were reduced to the necessity of killing our horses and mules, and living on them. We had nothing else of any kind whatever to eat but clear horse or mule meat, without even salt to salt it.

After passing the summit, and striking this stream, we worked our way along down for some distance, occasionally having to leave the track and go on to the ridges, to avoid getting into deep cañons, blocked with immense boulders. We got into some of these, and had to go back on to the ridges. We finally succeeded in working down to the north side of the river, and finding difficulty there, got on to the south side of the river. We went a little ways from the river, working down on that side, and passed I suppose the neighborhood of where Sonora is now.

Finally we got out of the mountains, striking the plains probably not far from where Knight's Ferry is now. When we got to the plains, we found no water or grass, it having been a dry season. That little stream we struck in the mountains proved to be what is now known as the Stanislaus River. We got on to the plains just at night, and followed down and camped about ten o'clock without water, and the next morning seeing a belt of timber to the north of us in the plain, we struck for that, our animals being much exhausted for want of water and feed, and it took us about all day to reach the place. We got into the belt of timber, and found a river there, the Stanislaus, the same that we had struck in the mountains. We found in that neighborhood signs of deer; so we agreed to stay there the next day, and go hunting. We did so, and killed several deer, and brought them into camp, and had a feast of fine venison.[20] Then we started to follow the river down, and after going a little way, we met two of our men who had left the party a number of days before in a cañon of the Stanislaus, and had worked their way down on foot ahead of us, and had reached Marsh's ranch at the foot of Mt. Diablo, and had told him of us back in the mountains, and he had furnished him with some Indians and animals and provisions, and fortunately, they just happened to meet us, and gave us the provisions, and we went on to the pass of the San Joaquin and to Marsh's ranch. That was the first settlement we reached in the country, about the 4th of November.[21]

Crossing the valley at that time, we saw immense herds of wild horses and elk running over the plain, and we had no further trouble about provisions. Marsh had got out here through New Mexico, I think, and came up the coast. Several men had been out trapping, and finally worked their way through Mexico, and got into the southern part of the country, and worked their way up the coast, and Marsh was one of them. He was called Dr. Marsh.[22] We stayed there a day or two, and a portion of the company left, and went from there to Sutter's Fort, which had been established a year or so before.[23]

About a dozen of us, after resting a day or so at Marsh's Ranch, started out to go down to the Pueblo San Jose, with directions from Marsh how to find our way there. We came on to that place, crossing what is now Livermore's Ranch, but there was no settlement there then.[24] We proceeded, and stopped one night at Geary's [Joaquin Higuera] ranch, two or three miles south of the mission of San Jose.[25] We excited a good deal of interest as we passed by the mission of San Jose, where there was a mission station, and some native Californians lived around there.

When we reached Geary's ranch, not being able to speak Spanish, we hardly knew how to get along; but we made signs that we wanted something to eat, whereupon they went out and lassoed a bullock, and threw it down, and cut its throat, and told us we could take the hide off, and cut off what we wanted to cook and eat. We camped there that night, and were very kindly treated by the people. When we got ready to go in the morning, we offered pay for the bullock, and they refused it.

The next morning [November 8], we started along the

road to San Jose. When we got to where the Coyote
Creek crosses the road, three miles out of the town, we
were met by a party of soldiers under an officer, who
had come out from the town to arrest us.[26] We could not
get any explanation of this movement, not being able to
speak the language. It appears that a report had preceded us that there was a large party of Americans behind us who had got into the country from the east, and
were going to raise a revolution, and take possession of
the country. Under this impression they had sent this
party out and made us prisoners. We were compelled to
submit to them, and allow ourselves to be captured, because, before leaving Marsh's ranch, he advised us to
leave our arms at his place, as he thought there might be
some trouble. So we could not make any resistance, and
were taken prisoners and carried into San Jose.

We were put into an old adobe building, and kept
under restraint, not closely confined, but watched, and
held under arrest for four or five days, I think, and then
were sent back to the mission of San Jose, under a guard,
and put into a building that had been used as a kind of
prison there, an old adobe building, and given quarters
there, and kept there, though not closely confined, for,
I think, about three days more. Meantime the authorities
had investigated the subject, and ascertained that there
were only about 30 of us altogether who had come into
the country, and there was no great danger of our taking
possession, we were so few in number, and so they finally
concluded to release us.[27] Alexander Forbes, however,
an Englishman living in that vicinity, then came in and
gave some kind of pledge for our good conduct, I think,
and said that we should not make any disturbance, and
upon that they set us free, and gave us passports to travel

through the country, wherever we saw fit to go.[28] We then dispersed from there, some going in one direction, and some in another.

During the winter prior to our arrival, there had been very little rain, and drought ensued, and but little was raised in the country, and there was scarcely any bread to be had, and people were living mainly upon beef. The country was bare of vegetation.[29] Everything was then in a very primitive condition. There was a pueblo at San Jose; it was a small village of perhaps three or four hundred people, with a few adobe houses, and what they called *pala parada*, houses consisting of posts standing upright in the ground, and then filled in with mud, and with a thatch of straw over the roof.[30] It was a very simple mode of life they lived. The people who had any wealth, had it in cattle, at their ranches around in the vicinity. They cultivated but very little grain, had small gardens which they called *milpitas*, where they raised vegetables in the summer. At that season, the families would go to the *milpitas,* put up a brush house, and raise a few things, —corn, beans, melons, peppers &c., and there were some small fields of corn, wheat and barley, where they raised in favorable seasons enough of these articles for their own use, the corn and wheat for bread stuffs, and the barley for feeding their horses. The lands surrounding the pueblo on the outside were alloted to families for cultivation, a small patch of ground which they called *suerte,* to each head of a family.

They were governed by an Alcalde generally, who exercised almost arbitrary power in civil affairs, and whose powers were judicial also. He acted as magistrate of the place, and mayor. Then there was generally an *ayuntamiento,* over which the alcalde presided, and all cases of dispute were tried before him. Criminal actions were tried before him also. Of course there were other judicial authorities above him, the Prefect for instance.[31]

I would say this in regard to my impression of the country: The people lived in a very primitive rude state. Although they had large houses, they were only partially floored; they usually contained one large room in the middle, for a kind of hall or general room, and small sleeping rooms, and at the end a kind of shed for the kitchen and cooking. Except in some of the best families, they did not generally have any table set in their rooms. They would commonly go into the kitchen and have the food taken from the kettles, and passed around in plates. Beef, beans and chili peppers were the chief articles of diet, and what they called *tortillas,* thin wafer-like cakes cooked on a piece of iron, made of corn or wheat flour. The better class of families would generally have a table on which the meat was set. The chief business was cattle raising, and the wealth of the country consisted of cattle; they also had a good many horses.

The commerce of the country was in hides and tallow. Every year, at the proper season, when the cattle were fat, along in July, August and September, they would have a *matanza;* that is, the ranchero would gather in the cattle to kill them, and kill off such number as they thought necessary to supply their wants by the sale of their hides and tallow. Some of the best of the meat would be cut off in strings, and dried or jerked, and that would be preserved to use along as they might require it; the main object of the killing, however, was to get their hides and tallow for sale. That was sold to the ships that came out here, from Boston mainly, with cargoes of goods, which they would sell to the rancheros at different points on the coast, taking their pay in hides and tallow. They brought dry goods, articles of clothing, groceries, wines and liquors, hardware, and most of the common necessaries of life. The people bought almost everything except beef and flour. They sometimes bought ready-made clothing, but generally purchased the cloth and made it up themselves into their style of clothing.

Alvarado was the Governor, and the capitol was at Monterey. The military branch was in command of Jose Castro in that district; the north side of the bay was in command of Ge.ⁿ Vallejo.[32] As near as I can recollect, I should think there were about 30 men under the direction of the military authority. They were armed, of course.

I judge there was considerable alarm amongst the authorities of the country about the time we arrived, from what I learned, perhaps not very extensive among the people. I think this idea of interference which they entertained arose from the fact that one or two years before, in 1839 or '40, there had been reports in the country here in circulation, that the foreign residents here, Americans and English, who were denominated foreigners, a few of whom were scattered through the country, had designs of this kind. At the time the revolution occurred here, which I think was in '38, in which the regular Mexican Governor was driven out, and Alvarado was made Governor, some of the Americans and other foreign residents joined the Alvarado party and assisted them in the revolution.[33] Most of these men were armed with the old-fashioned western hunting rifles, and employed in the conflict as sharpshooters, and they made such effective use of their weapons, that the people regarded them with considerable apprehension and dread. After Alvarado was made Governor, I think in the latter part of '39 or '40, a report was put

in circulation that the Americans and other foreign residents were conspiring together to raise another revolution
in the country against Alvarado, and in apprehension of
what these men might do, the authorities made arrangements to arrest pretty much all the foreign residents in
the country, and did so arrest them, and make them
prisoners, and send them out of the country, some to San
Blas. This was by order of the Governor. There might
have been fifty or so thus sent away. This was in Monterey County, and at San Jose and Los Angeles.[34]

Among them was Capt. Graham, who was living at
that time at Natividad, on the Salinas plains. He was
somewhat of a prominent man among the Americans, and
the Californians looked upon him as rather a leader in
this movement which they thought was impending. I do
not think there was any real intention on the part of the
Americans to make a movement of this kind, but they
talked like Americans, and had not a very high appreciation of the military arm of the government, and probably
they boasted about what they could do, and the natives took
the alarm from this. They were kept there several months,
I think, under restraint. When Graham was arrested, he
and Henry Neil [Naile] were living together, and I think
were running a distillery at Natividad, and the Californians came upon them in the night and attacked them, and
took them prisoners, as they were a much superior force.
Graham was an American and had taken part in the
movement by which Alvarado had been put in power; he
and other foreigners joined the Alvarado movement in a
little company by themselves, and helped him and his
force in their revolutionary designs. I think at the time
that was going on, that the old fort outside of the town of
Monterey had some cannon, and the Alvarado party got

possession of the premises, and I have heard it said that Graham or some other of the Americans loaded one of the pieces and sighted it, and pointed it towards the town and fired it, and the ball struck the roof of the Governor's house in town, and tore away a portion of it, and upon that the forces in town got alarmed, and finally surrendered to the Alvarado party. After some months the prisoners at San Blas were released, and most of them returned, some to their old places; and Graham and Neil [Naile] came back to establish themselves at a ranch called *Cyant* [Sayante], near Santa Cruz, and built a saw mill there.[35]

When our party came into the country, I suppose, from the fact that these troubles had occurred with the American residents here before, the Governor probably imagined that there might be contemplated some concerted action, which included the entry of our party into the country, to take possession of it, and that we were to join with the people already here for that purpose, and so, as a matter of precaution, they arrested us, as before stated.

After we were released, Mr. Brolask[i] and myself went out to Marsh's ranch, and got our guns and the things we had left there, and then returned to the Pueblo San Jose; others scattered to different parts of the country, and I don't know where they went. We stopped there a few days at the house of a Scotchman who lived there Farquharson or Ferguson, who lived with a Spanish woman, and had a family there.[36]

There is a little incident I remember, which will illustrate how things were done in those days. When we arrived there, we placed our horses which we rode in charge of a native Californian that Ferguson had in the house, and he kept them in the corral for several days while we stayed there, up to the night previous to the morning when we intended to leave, to go to Santa Cruz. On that morning, when we were ready to start on our journey, we found our horses missing, and we had a strong suspicion that the man who had charge of them had driven them away himself, so that we could not find them, thus imposing on us the necessity of hiring other horses from him to take us on our journey. We had to hire them accordingly, and lost our own. Of course, we had no proof, but were pretty well satisfied that that was the way it happened. He furnished us with horses, and started with us, and the horses on which we were mounted were thin and poor, like most other horses in that dry season. We rode some four or five miles out of San Jose into the country, and this man then represented that the horses could not perform the journey, stopped there, and lassoed some other horses, and brought them in, some which he had found about there, not belonging to him. We then took them, and made the journey over to Santa Cruz. They would just lasso any horse on the road, and on returning they would perhaps exchange again.

Brolask[i] and I went to Capt. Graham's place at Cyant [Sayante], near Santa Cruz, and on arriving there we found some little excitement among the few Americans around there, they having heard of the arrival of our party, and of our having been made prisoners. A man by the name of Daniel Majors was there in that neighborhood, and another by the name of Wm Ware.[37] They had talked the matter over among themselves, and had thought of raising what little force of foreign residents they could, and coming over to San Jose and making an attempt to release us. They might not have done it, but it showed the feeling that existed at that time.

There was not much education among the people. The better class could read and write, but the common class of people were very deficient in education. They had little schools about the missions, and got some instruction there but very limited. Their amusements consisted chiefly of fandangoes.[38] Almost every night where there was any settlement of people, there would be a fandango and dancing. There was a good deal of horse racing, some cock fighting, and bull and bear fighting also. They were a very primitive, simple-minded people, but very shrewd naturally, and lived in a very primitive simple way, most of them, and though there was a good deal of difference in families, some being wealthy, and others not, yet there was a good deal of democratic feeling among the people; that is, there was not much distinction of different classes, not a strong aristocratic feeling; that is, the wealthy did not despise the lower classes. Whenever there was a dance or fandango in any of the villages, most of the people would come in. In the large houses, there was a large hall or room in the middle, and dances would be held there, sometime in one house, sometimes another. Their music consisted mainly of the guitar and violin, and they performed very well on them, simple tunes and dance music. A good many of the people played on these instruments.

They were a very hospitable people as a general thing, so much so that a man could travel all over the country without a cent of money, if necessary. Every man travelling carried his serrappa [serapa] or Mexican blanket with him, which served in rainy or cold weather, and at night was a covering to sleep under; and a man travelling could stop at any house where night overtook him, and was welcome to such accommodation as they could afford, generally a hide to lie on in the common houses, and a simple bed in the better class, and his food was always given with good will, and without any charge whatever. If his horse was tired and could not go any farther, they would generally allow him to leave the horse, and furnish him with another to continue his journey, with the understanding that on returning he would exchange the horse again. This applied to anybody that came along, whether of their own nationality or strangers. If they had no room in the house, they would furnish him with a hide, and give him his food without pay.

Many of these ranches were very extensive. There were but few towns of any size. Monterey and San Jose were the principal towns, and near Santa Cruz there was a little village called Branciforte; but most of the other settlements were the mission settlements, around which were collected a number of people, making a kind of village, independent of the mission Indians. The people who had herds of cattle depended upon them for their support. The poorer classes of people who had no stock of their own were generally employed as vaqueros to handle their stock and work in the matanzas, and to some extent in cultivation, but very slightly. They generally had their little milpitas, or gardens. The princip[le] work was done, though, by what were called amongst them the *gente de rason,* (people of reason, it means literally), as distinguished from the Indians. The poorer class of these people were employed mainly in working with stock, handling them, taking care of them, marking and branding and killing them. The poorest labor was performed by the Indians who had been brought in from the mountains and somewhat Christianized and civilized by the missions, and when the missions were finally broken up, the Indians were employed by the rancheros.

I have often remarked, in speaking of these people, that I thought at that time they were the happiest and most contented class of people I had ever seen, were more free from care, anxiety and trouble than any people I ever knew. There was some dissipation among them, drinking and gambling, the latter almost a universal vice. The better class gambled not so much as the poorer part of the population. The common people could frequently be seen sitting in a ring on the ground, playing cards for anything they had. If they had no money, they would bet away portions of their clothing, a horse or saddle, or anything they could command. The wealthier class of people were very liberal, and there was no trouble about anybody's getting enough to eat, and when they killed a bullock, which they did frequently, the poorer people who had no cattle would come up and get a portion of the meat, which was given freely; so there was no destitution among them. The common class of people had very little thought of the future; they lived to enjoy the present day, and seemed to have very little ambition to accumulate anything; there was indeed scarcely anything to accumulate. They lived to enjoy themselves in their way, and were happy and contented, free from care, and the struggles and strifes and ambition to accumulate or change their condition.

When the rancheros had a matanza, which means the killing of a lot of cattle once a year, when they were fat, he would have a lot of cattle brought up and placed in corrals near the house somewhere, and then those in the best condition to kill were selected from the band, and slaughtered, their hides taken off, staked out, and dried for sale, the tallow was tried out and run into bags made of bullocks' hides sewed up, making what was called a *bota* of tallow. After slaughtering a lot of cattle sufficient to furnish as many hides and as much tallow as was required to supply the family with such goods as they needed to purchase, for the year generally, the remainder of the cattle were returned to the general herds. The hides formed in one sense the currency of the country, and were the medium of exchange for what they wanted to purchase, a hide always being reckoned at $2—, without any reference to the size or weight of it, and they were taken in trade at that valuation; and the tallow was generally sold for about $1.50 an asoba [*sic*], that being about 25 pounds weight. When a man bought goods on credit, the understanding was, as a general thing, that he was to pay in hides at $2— each, and tallow at $1.50 an asoba.[39] Some of the people had small stores, with small stocks of goods. There were no taxes to amount to anything except customs duties, which were very high. There was a Custom House at Monterey, where all vessels had to enter.[40] There was a heavy tax on imported liquor, but no internal tax on the *arguadiente* [aguardiente] the native brandy made from grapes, which was the common stimulating drink among the people.[41]

Most of the trade of the country was barter trade; there was very little money in the country. The goods were bought mostly from vessels which came from Boston for cargoes of hides. This trade commenced several years before I came here. The merchants bought the goods of the vessels with the understanding that they were to pay in hides and tallow, and they sold them at retail for the same kind of currency with which they paid the bills to the ships. The ships made trips to the different parts of the coast and collected hides, and generally took them to San Diego, and salted and prepared them for shipment on the vessel when she had collected enough for a full cargo.[42]

The most of the country was occupied with stock ranches, consisting of from one to eight or ten leagues each, as the case might be. These ranches were held under free grants from the Mexican Government to heads of families, without any cost, except the expense of getting the papers made out, & some little office expenses, perhaps some fifty or sixty dollars in all.

A pretty large portion of the country at that time was occupied by the missions, embraced within the lands appropriated to their use. Each mission had grants, and a large stock of cattle and horses, and some sheep. They were subject to the control of the government, and under its protection, although the padres had pretty much command of the missions, each one where he was located, and charge of the Indians attached thereto. Some of the missions had at one time from two to seven or eight hundred Indians. They were given lands and privileges for the purpose of Christianizing the Indians, and carrying on missionary work. There was a church in San Jose, and one in Monterey, and another in Los Angeles, independent of the missions, all Catholic Churches. A mission was generally managed by one friar or padre. Some of them were very good men, most of them I presume were, and there were some exceptions, some bad and licen[t]ious.

I think their influence over the Indians generally was pretty good, and they succeeded to a considerable extent in civilizing and Christianizing them. In some instances the Indians became dissatisfied, and went back into the mountains. When trained, they became good vaqueros and skillful in handling stock and cultivating the soil. At the missions, enough ground was cultivated to supply them with grain for their own use, and at one time they sold some wheat to the Russians on the north coast.[43] The missions had been mainly under the charge of the priests and padres, but I think somewhere about the time I came here, or a little after, they were secularized, as it was called, and put under the control of a mayordomo appointed by the government, a kind of superintendent, who had a general oversight of the missions. The priests after that were confined more to the clerical duties of the missions. Finally some of the mission lands were divided up and sold into ranches before they were entirely abandoned. The Indians began to leave, and they gradually were broken up, and some of the lands were divided up and granted or sold to some of the favorites of the government for a nominal consideration. The missions accumulated some wealth, in herds of cattle or horses, which belonged to the church in general, not to the priests individually.

Sutter established his fort about '39 or '40, I think. I think he bought the stock and farming implements of the Russians, and established his fort on the Sacramento River.[44] I think this Russian establishment was a fur company, and they had hunters about the coast and interior, and they made it a source of obtaining supplies of wheat in earlier years. They used to collect wheat which they bought there, and sent it up to Alaska.[45] When we went into Marsh's ranch first, some of our party went from there to Sutter's Fort.[46]

From Graham's place, Mr. Brolask[i] and I, after staying a few days, went into Monterey, and I stayed there a little while, and there I became acquainted with Mr. Larkin, who was afterwards American Consul, and made arrangements with him to go over to Santa Cruz and take charge of a store there, which he wished to establish as a branch, and so I went over to manage the business there for him,—a store of general merchandise. We carried on the usual business there, selling goods and taking pay in hides and tallow, and buying lumber.[47] At that time Graham and Neil [Naile] had their sawmill at Cyant [Sayante], and there were a number of men in the mountains out of Santa Cruz, sawing lumber in sawpits by hand. I bought the lumber of them, and had it hauled on to the beach, taking it in exchange for goods, and sold it to the ships that came in, in exchange for goods, and they sold it down the coast at different points where it was required. This was mostly the redwood lumber, and was worth about forty or forty-five dollars a thousand then.[48] We used also to have some trade in a kind of soap that was made in the country, taking it from the manufacturers, and retailing it around to the people in exchange for hides, and sometimes delivered some of it to the ships in exchange for goods.

In taking the hides from the country people in exchange for goods, we had the regulation that all hides must be branded before they were sold, with the owner's brand, to show that they had not been stolen. The owners were all known, and each had a recognized brand, and the brand had to be put on them. After gathering a quantity of hides when I wanted to deliver them to the ship, the Alcalde would always come and overhaul them, and see if they were properly branded, and if not, they were seized by him and confiscated. I recollect that in one case I had considerable trouble with the Alcalde. In some instances a man would bring a hide in, and had perhaps forgotten to brand it, and there might be some hides collected in that way. They would promise to come in and brand them afterwards, but perhaps neglected to do it. In the case I speak of, I had a considerable number without the brands on, which had been gathered in this way, and I was expecting to make a shipment, and on account of the hides with no brands on, I did not care to have the Alcalde overhaul them, and so I made arrangements with the ship to have them taken away very early one morning, and locked up the store and went away, so that the Alcalde should not come and overhaul them that afternoon. I made arrangements to get them down to the beach in carts about daylight the next morning. When I got them down there, I found there was no boat to take them off. I did not know what to do, but having a lot of lumber there, I had the hides packed in a pile under a bank, and covered up with lumber, to wait until the boat should come ashore. In the meantime the Alcalde got wind of the hides having gone down, and came charging down to the beach, mad as could be, and wanted to know where the hides were. I told him he was too late, that I had to send them down to the ship early, as she wanted to go off. After he had stormed about for some time, I got the supercargo of the vessel to take the Alcalde off to the mission, on some pretence or other, and while he had him up there, I got the men to haul the hides out from under the lumber, and put them aboard the ship. There was no penalty for shipping them without supervision, if we could manage to do so.[49]

Speaking about the character of the priests, at the mission of Santa Cruz, the priest broke open my store, and robbed me of a considerable amount of goods, while I was away on one occasion. I rented the store of him, and it was a part of the mission buildings. It opened on the rear of the courtyard, on which his office also opened. One day on returning from the country, I found the store had been broken open in the rear, and that a considerable lot of goods of various kinds had disappeared. I had some suspicion of him, and put myself on the watch, to see if I could find anything to prove it. After awhile, the woman at the house where he lived came into the store one day, and asked me how I came to sell rotten calico to the padre. I told her I did not know I had sold him any rotten calico. She said, yes, I had, a whole piece of it, and it was very bad and rotten. I asked her what kind of calico it was, and she pointed to a piece on the shelves, and said it was like that. There were two pieces of this kind, and one had been taken at the time of the robbery. This showed me at once who had taken the goods away. I told her I believed that calico had been injured in the coloring, but I did not remember having sold any of it, and if she would bring the bolt of calico back, I would exchange it, and give her another piece. She was pleased with that, but after she [saw the] priest, she never came to make the exchange. The padre was held to be above law under the Mexican government, and if I had brought the charge of robbery against him, he might have made me a great deal of trouble, and have done me much injury, as he had a good deal of influence with the people. So, under the circumstances I let the matter go, and never made any complaint. I afterwards saw some colored handkerchiefs, which were missing from my store after the robbery, hung out of the window of the mission on the occasion of some religious holiday. This priest was fond of gambling and drinking also.[50]

I continued there about two and a half years in that kind of trade & selling goods. Finally, after having accumulated a large quantity of lumber that I had no sale for, at the beach, some 150 thousand feet more than I could dispose of, I stopped buying, and the sawyers, as I supposed, in order to make a new market for lumber, when

I was gone into Monterey on one occasion, set fire to the lumber and burned it up, and this disgusted Mr. Larkin so much that he closed the business up, and I went into Monterey.[51]

Before I went into Monterey, while I was living in Santa Cruz, in '42 I think it was, Com. [Thomas] Ap Catesby Jones came into the harbor in the flag ship, and under a report that he had of approaching war between the United States and Mexico, he landed his marines and took possession of Monterey, and raised the American flag there, and sent an officer out to Santa Cruz and raised the flag there under proclamation, and appointed me as Alcalde under the American government, to exercise the office there. In a day or two, however, news was received that it was all a mistake, and Jones had given up the possession of Monterey and retired to the ship, and that we would have to take down the flag and restore the government to the authorities. We immediately did so. The Californians did not attempt to make any opposition. They talked a good deal, and blowed round, but made no trouble otherwise.[52]

A man by the name of Dawson who came in the company I did, opened a little store at Santa Cruz while I was there, and presently closed it and went away.[53] There was an Englishman, W.[m] Thompson, living at the mission, married to a California woman, and he was the only foreigner there.[54] At Cyant [Sayante] there were Graham and Majors. In the hills around there were a number of men sawing lumber, mainly sailors who had drifted in from vessels. There was a man by the name of Michael Lodge, a little ways from the town, on a ranch who was the father of Mrs. Thos. Fallon.[55]

In regard to Jose [de] Jesus Vallejo, who was living

near the mission at the time, on the north side of the bay, when we were prisoners at San Jose, he used to send us meat and provisions, and one thing and another, and seemed disposed to do what he could to make our condition as comfortable as could be, and I think had some influence in getting our release.[56]

Some time after I had gone to Monterey, in '44 I think it was, and was keeping store there, the revolution against Micheltoren[a] commenced. He was in command there and had a garrison. He had been sent out as Governor to supersede Alvarado. The revolution against him was raised by the native Californians, with a view of superseding him. He first came to Los Angeles and held possession there, and afterwards moved to Monterey, and had a garrison and military force and officers there. It was a general movement of the native Californians to drive him out, and put a native Californian in his place. They banded together and raised a force, and Sutter got a lot of Americans up the Sacramento Valley who joined with the Micheltoren[a] party against the Californians, and after some skirmishing about the northern part of the country, they gathered their forces down south. They fought a battle at Canuga [Chuenga].[57]

While Micheltoren[a] was gone down south with his forces, he left his wife there in charge of his house at Monterey, the Government house and office and headquarters, and left an officer with a company of Mexican soldiers there, to protect Monterey against any attack of the native Californians, and after he had got some way down south, the Californians got up a party round the country, numbering some eighty or a hundred men, and marched in toward Monterey to take that place. When they got within two or three miles of the town, they made a camp there, and sent in a demand for the surrender of the town. In the meantime, however, before this occurred, Mrs. Micheltoren[a], the Governor's wife, had become afraid of her own soldiers, who were a very hard set, a good many of them having come from Mexico as convicts from the prisons there, and she became fearful that they might revolt, and perhaps plunder her own house, and so she went to Mr. Larkin, the American Consul, and asked him if he could not get some Americans to come to her house and act as a guard during the night, for fear the soldiers might make a break upon the house and take possession. Upon that request, Mr. Larkin came to me, and asked me if I could get a few Americans to act as a guard, with good arms. So I got some five or six Americans, and we armed ourselves well with American rifles, and went there. Mrs. Micheltoren[a] had a room fitted up for us, a kind of armory, and we went and stayed there every night, for four or five weeks, I think, and kept guard, to protect the house, and the public property in the offices there.[58]

While we were doing that, this party of Californians came in near the town, as before stated, and camped, and sent in to demand the surrender of the town. Upon that, Mrs. Micheltoren[a] called a council in her house of the officer in charge and some of the leading citizens there, to consider what was best to be done. After considerable discussion, the general opinion seemed to be in favor of surrendering the place, rather than taking the risk of their making an attack upon it, and perhaps causing the loss of life and property. After this discussion, Mrs. Micheltoren[a] came out in the room, and made an address to the people assembled there, and told them she had been left in charge of the house and public offices there by her husband, while he was away south, and she protested against their being delivered up to the attacking party, and made quite a patriotic and stirring speech, insisting that the place should not be surrendered, and said if they would not defend her, that she had some friends who were coming to her house for its protection every night, and she would defend it, with their aid, to the last extremity; and she talked so boldly and bravely that she quite shamed those who were in favor of surrender, and they finally came to her opinion, and decided to assist her in holding the place. She then sent to me, and I got the others, and we went up the[re] with our arms, and she sent word out to the invading party that the place would not be surrendered, and they sent back word allowing so many hours to surrender. In the meantime, some persons went out to the camp of the Californians, and represented to them that the house would be well defended if attacked, and there might be considerable bloodshed, and advised them not to make the attack. Finally an agreement was negotiated between the Commissioners sent out by Mrs. Micheltoren[a] and the Californians to the effect that they might march round to the rear of the town, and take possession of the old fort on the north side of the town above the bay, and hold possession of the fort, and the Governor's wife should hold the city, until such time as intelligence could be obtained of the result of the action down in the southern part of the country, with the further understanding that if Micheltoren[a] was defeated in that quarter, the Californians should be allowed to come in and take charge of the town; and, on the other hand, if the Californians were defeated down south, then the Californians should retire from the town, and make no further demonstration against it. That arrangement was carried into effect, and everything remained quiet for a few days, until news finally came that Micheltoren[a] had been defeated below, and had agreed to retire from the governorship, and give it up to the Californians, and arrangements were made for Pio Pico to take his place as Governor. After that, Micheltoren[a] came back to settle up the affairs of the government, and the office was transferred to Pico for the Californians, and Micheltoren[a] retired to Mexico.[59] For my agency there in protecting his house, I got the title to a grant of land completed which I had applied for, on the Sacramento River.[60]

Monterey at that time, and previous to his going away, had been the headquarters of the Government, and was quite a lively and gay place. There was considerable population there, and quite a garrison of soldiers and officers, and these, in connection with the government patronage, made quite a lively place. There was a good deal of amusement and life there, and it was more of a place than it has ever been since. Under Pico, the seat of Government was transferred to Los Angeles, and Monterey began to decline.

At the time Larkin was carrying on business in Monterey, he had a good deal of influence there, because he acted as the financial advisor of Micheltoren[a], and assisted him in getting supplies &c. They consulted him a good deal in regard to the government, and placed a good deal of confidence in him. I think Micheltoren[a] was a pretty good governor; I dont think there was much objection to him; but his troops at Monterey were a very hard set; they stole and were fighting amongst themselves, and committed all sorts of outrages, would get up broils and troubles, and were very apt to commit violence with their knives, cutting each other and other people and were a bad set generally, a great portion of them having been convicts in Mexico, and released on condition that they would become soldiers; they were very disagreeable with the native population, overbearing and insolent. There was a prejudice in the minds of the native Californians against being under the control of the Mexican Government. They wanted control of the government in their own people, and in addition they were very much incensed against the soldiery sent here to uphold the Mexican authority. The wife of Micheltoren[a] was a very nice, bright, intelligent woman, brave as could be. She pleased me very much in her action against delivering up the town. A number among the American and foreign residents were there, Hartnell, Cooper, and others.[61]

A company came out to this coast by the southern route, not long after our company came, consisting of the following persons:—W.[m] Workman, John Ro[w]land, Benito [Benjamin] D. Wilson, Albert G. Toomes, W.[m] Knight, W.[m] Gordon, W.[m] Moore, Isaac Given,—Pickman, Fred.[k] Bachelor,—Teabo [Tibeau], Wade Hampton, D.[r] [James A.] Mead, D.[r] [Wm.] Gamble, Hiram Taylor, [Thomas] Lindsay, Col. [John]M.[c] Clure. They came through New Mexico, and stopped mostly about Los Angeles, I think.[62]

Some of the emigrants who crossed with me went back the next Spring, about half the party. They went south, out through Walker's Pass, and by some southern route, I rather think through New Mexico. Some of the second colony also went back.[63] Mr Toomes, with whom I became intimately acquainted, got a grant of land at Tehama.[64] Wilson and Ro[w]land and Workman settled at Los Angeles. Some came in '43, I think,—Major Hixley [Hensley], Major Rich, Major Snyder, and also Black-

burn, who died at Santa Cruz. Some of them were at
Monterey.[65] In '44 I think there was a party came in,
and one in '46.[66] After the arrival of our party, I dont
think there was any difficulty between those who came and
the native Californians. They did not seem to have much
apprehension of the new comers until along in 1846, when
there was considerable emigration came in; then the same
trouble was felt.

I dont know anything about the Bear Flag personally,
only by report. The movement commenced on the north
side of the bay amongst the foreigners who were settled
there, and they professed to think, I believe, over there,
that the California authorities were going to send a party
of men to drive them out. There were not a great many,
but some round in Napa, Sonoma, Cash Creek, and between Sacramento and Sonoma. They got together some
30 or 40 men, I think from different quarters, round up
towards Sacramento, and formed a kind of company there,
and then came down to Sonoma, and took some of the
leading Californians prisoners who lived in that vicinity.
Gen. Vallejo, the military commander of that northern
country, lived there; but I think he had no military force
there. I think they collected about Sutter's Fort, and then
came down to Sonoma and took possession of that place,
and took Salvador Vallejo and Victor Prudon prisoners.
They merely took possession and held the place, and
issued a Proclamation of Independence, and raised the
Bear Flag, intending to establish an independent government there. A man by the name of [Ezekiel] Merritt, I
think, was at the head of it first. He went off with a party
who expected to come up from Monterey.[67]

After they took Sonoma and the prisoners, I think, a
party of them started out towards Sutter's Ft., with a

view of intercepting a party of Californians who were expected up that way to collect horses and take them to Monterey, and who were fitting out an expedition to test the possession of the country with the Americans who had taken it. The Bear Flag men who started out from Sonoma did so, I think, with a view of finding these Californians, and taking their horses away from them. When Merrit[t] left there, a man by the name of [William B.] Ide, a Mormon, was put at the head of affairs, and he raised the flag and issued this proclamation.[68]

In the meantime, the Californians had collected a party of men over across the bay on this side, and a detachment of the main [American] force at Sonoma sent out a couple of men to reconnoitre, and they were caught and murdered by this party of Californians. I think a man by the name of Fowler was one. They caught them and tied them to trees, and shot them, as spies probably.[69] I think the party at Sonoma sent out 10, 15 or 20 men, when they heard of this massacre, to see if they could overtake the party of Californians and defeat them. I am not sure whether they came in contact with them; I rather think they retreated and got away.[70]

The result of it was that after they took possession of Sonoma, and issued their proclamation, and raised their flag; the movement came to a sudden termination in this way: Fremont was in the country then, down south, and had started up north with his party of explorers, having been rather ordered out of the country by the authorities, and the party at Sonoma sent out to him a dispatch for him to join them; but before he got back there, the news came of the declaration of war between the United States and Mexico, and the American flag was hoisted at Monterey, and the parties at Sonoma gave up their organiza-

tion under the Bear Flag, and Fremont came back, and
some of them joined him to carry on the war against Mexico under the U.S. Government. They held possession of
Sonoma perhaps three or four weeks.[71]

After the arrival of our party and we had been made
prisoners and released, there did not seem to be any
opposition made against Americans until 1846, when there
were getting to be considerable numbers of them, and the
authorities then began to fear they were too strong, and
there began to be some talk about prohibiting any further
emigration, and of getting rid of those who were here.
There was perhaps some little feeling of jealousy existing
before that, occasioned by the Americans coming in, but
no active measures were taken to prevent them from
coming.

When Fremont came in here the last time, in the latter
part of '45 I think, he brought in his company of explorers,
and went down to Monterey or near there, to San Juan,
and the authorities then raised some opposition to his
coming into the country with armed men, in the way he
did, and I believe ordered him to leave the country. A
dispute arose between him and them; I think that he
wanted the privilege to go into Monterey, and that was
refused him, and some dispute arose, and they then ordered
him to leave the country with his party, he being somewhere in the neighborhood of San Juan, and he, antici-
pating that some active measures might be taken to force
him to leave the country, took his troops and went into
Gavilan Mountain, a few miles south of the mission of
San Juan, and to some extent entrenched himself there
in a secure position, so that he might be able to defend
himself against any attack they might make on him. I
think they collected some force at San Juan or Monterey,

and made some demonstrations towards driving him out, but probably came to the conclusion that they had better not make any attack on him there. After remaining there some time, and finding that he was not attacked, and aware that he would not be allowed to go into Monterey, he finally got such supplies as he required for his journey, and retired from the position he had held in the Gavilan mountain, and commenced his march up north, and had got some distance up the Sacramento Valley, when this disturbance broke out at Sonoma.[72]

I never thought a great deal of Fremont, and I thought generally he was overestimated as to his ability and capacity. He became very vain and conceited in his own estimation. Of course he became somewhat prominent. During the war, he pretended to act as Governor at Los Angeles, before the matter was settled, but he was suspended by orders from Gen. Kearny. He had a difficulty with Gen. Mason, and I believe was courtmartialed and superseded and sent home. I think he was not tried.[73] He came out here afterward and brought his wife, and was at San Jose at the meeting of the legislature, and was elected U.S. Senator, and served for a short time, he having been chosen for the short term.[74]

It was said that there was a scheme on foot, supposed to be under English influence and auspices, for a man named McNamara to come here and get possession of a large portion of the San Joaquin Valley. I think he was coming here from some part of Mexico, probably Monterey. It was thought the English government were working to get a foothold here. The idea I think was to get a large concession of land to him from the Mexican Government, in the interior of the country, near the San Joaquin Valley, and by that means for the English

Government to get a hold here, and thus get some advantage in the country. Some of this was probable, but I dont know whether any such thing was ever really thought of.[75]

At the time the war commenced, it was understood that an English frigate, the Collin[g]wood, was coming here. She started from San Blas or Mazatlan, with a view of getting possession of Monterey, to assume a protectorate, before the American fleet could get in here and take possession of Monterey first after war was declared, but the American commander beat her in getting here and took possession. That was supposed to have been the design, but I dont know that there is any proof that it really was.[76] All the foreigners were greatly rejoiced, when war was declared, at the prospect of the country's coming under the American government. The natives of course were very much displeased with it, and made what resistance they could, but it did not amount to much.

In the latter part of '44, I went to Monterey, and kept a little store there until the fall of '45, and then got a grant of land up on the Sacramento River from the Mexican Government. When the Californians took possession of the government under Pico, after Micheltoren[a] retired, and the seat of government was transferred to Los Angeles, Monterey rather declined. In that year, along in the summer of '45, a vessel came up the coast, from England, with a cargo of goods belonging to John Parrott, who was doing business at Mazatlan then. He sent the vessel up to Monterey, and in endeavoring to get into the harbor, she got caught in a fog, and was wrecked on Pt. Lobos, near Carmel Bay, and sunk, and the whole cargo, which was valuable, was lost. Afterwards Mr. Parrott came up there, and the wreck and cargo were sold

on the spot, and five or six others associated with me purchased them. We then went to work, with boats and
grappling hooks, and one thing and another, and got up
a considerable quantity of the goods from the hull of the
vessel. They were all wet, but not much damaged otherwise. We secured in this way a large number of bales of
prints, calicoes, and linen cloth, and some silks, dry goods
generally, and spread them out on the beach to dry, and
sold them for whatever we could get, and realized a profit
on the venture.[77]

After war was declared, the feelings of the Californians
were hostile toward the Americans; they fought us as long
as they could. That in some measure died away among the
common class of people, but those who held lands and
property still felt a good deal of hostility, on account of
the difficulty of getting their titles after the war was ended.
As a general thing there was no bitter feeling; they
mixed together on good terms after the war was over. At
the time I was living in Monterey.

In '44 or '45, I wanted to get a grant of land with some
of my friends, and some of them explored the upper part
of the Sacramento valley to see what land was desirable
there for stock ranches. In order to get grants we had to
become naturalized as Mexican citizens. There was no
trouble about it; it was a formal thing. I merely got a man
there to write out a petition or application for papers of
naturalization, and by presenting it and waiting while
the papers were issued to me, and to others the same. I did
not go forward to take any oath of allegiance, but merely
had a written application, presented it, and after awhile
I got my papers which made me a Mexican citizen. After
that I was eligible to obtain a grant of land. It was simply
a free grant for four leagues of land, according to my

application, which amounted to about 18,000 acres. The grant was issued.[78] After these grants came into our hands, an Act of Congress was passed, requiring all such grants to be brought before a commission appointed for that purpose, sent out here in 1851. Most of these grants that were legal were confirmed; but some few that were not legal were also confirmed; but the attempts to get their titles thus confirmed involved the claimants in large expense. It was rather an unfortunate law, because it kept the land title in unsettled condition for many years, before anybody could purchase or secure the title to these lands. Doubtless it induced squatting on the land, and that made new litigation, and engendered bad feeling, and some lives were lost from this cause. The settlement of the country was retarded very much, I think, from the fact that the land titles were kept in uncertainty for a long time, and a great many who would have bought land here, seeing that the titles were doubtful, took their money east; and the men who squatted on the land, uncertain whether they would get any titles, were afraid to make any improvements, not feeling at all sure they could hold their possessions; and thus the development of the country was delayed for many years. All the Mexican grants were in trouble. They passed through the Board of Commissioners, and after their decision, the parties feeling themselves aggrieved appealed the cases to the District Court, and from that to the Supreme Ct. The expenses were very heavy, and the Californians in many instances had to give away a large portion of their land in order to get their titles finally confirmed. Most of the native Californians lost their land in that way.

In the fall of '45, I went upon the ranch on the Sacramento River, near Red Bluffs, and took some cattle up

there to stock it. I spent the winter of '45 and '46 there.[79]
I stopped at a place where Tehama is now. There was
a log cabin there owned by Mr. [Albert] Toomes, who
had a ranch there, and just as I got there, the rain set in,
and the whole country was overflowed, and we could not
travel to get back, and we stayed there in the log cabin,
two families, and three men of us besides, and spent the
winter there, and could not do much of anything outside,
the country was so full of water. In the latter part of the
winter, a man who first went up with me and I cut down
a big sycamore tree, and dug it out, and made a big canoe
out of it, and put our things into it, and came all the way
down to San Pablo Bay, and landed there just above the
point between this bay and San Pablo Bay, where we
hired some horses and went down to Monterey. That was
in the spring of '46.[80]

After a short time, I made an arrangement with Capt.
John Paty, who had a vessel trading on the coast, to go
to San Francisco and take charge of a store for him which
he wanted to establish for the sale of goods which he had
brought on his vessel. I opened a store on Dupont St. between Clay and Washington, in a large adobe building,
for general merchandise.[81] There were but very few
inhabitants here then. It was then called Yerba Buena,
and was simply a landing place where vessels came in
to lie and ship hides and deliver goods. There were some
fifteen or twenty houses of all kinds in the place, mostly
small shanties. The people were perhaps half Californians, and half foreigners. There were probably, of all kinds
and ages, about 150. Occasionally a vessel came here,
and once in a while two or three at a time; there were one
or two trading between here and the Sandwich Islands;
Capt. Paty's vessel came from there.[82] They got goods

at the Islands which had been brought there from other places and entered free of duty, and brought them over here.[83] There was one vessel from Callao and Valparaiso. They would take hides and tallow here, and the Boston ships also took hides and tallow in trade, and the vessel from the South American ports would exchange with the Boston vessel, taking tallow, and giving the Boston vessel hides.[84]

I carried on trade here for about a year, sold goods on credit, collected hides and tallow round the bay, sending launches out for this purpose, and then Captain Paty came to the conclusion that he would give up his business on the coast, as it did not meet his expectations here, and he gave it up accordingly, in 1846.[85]

Then I engaged for awhile after that in making collections for Wm H. Davis, round the country. He had a vessel here from the Sandwich Islands, and sold the goods, and engaged with me for a few months. That was in '47.[86]

After I got through with his business, I went down the coast, to Los Angeles and San Diego, and returned here in the Spring of '48, and then made arrangements with Howard & Mellus to establish a store in San Jose in partnership with them, and commenced business there in the spring of '48.[87] Shortly after I had opened my store and got everything started to go on and do business, the gold excitement commenced, and most of the men there started away to the mines. A good many families also left entirely, and I was left there with my stock of goods just opened, without hardly any people for customers, and the town almost depopulated.

Finding I could not do any business, I of course concluded to make a trip to the mines, and see what was going on there. I got an old gentleman by the name of Brenham to come into the store and look after it, while I should go up to the mines and look around.[88] I went up to the mining region about where Placerville is now, stayed there a few days, took observations, and started to return to San Jose. In the meantime, while I was away, a considerable number of the Spanish population, who had been in the mines from San Jose, and most of whom had succeeded in getting quite a quantity of gold, returned to that place, and with their newly acquired wealth had gone into the store to buy goods of Brenham, and were very eager to get goods for their gold, seeming to have a kind of apprehension that the gold would lose its value, and were anxious to realize something from it as soon as possible. They commenced trading at such a rate that I found on my return the man I had left in charge had sold out nearly my whole stock of goods. I had been gone some two or three weeks. From that time on I had frequently to renew my stock of goods from San Francisco, and the Spanish people coming in from the mines were anxious to trade. Money was rather a new thing to them, and having come easy and quickly, they were just as ready to spend it, and having a fancy for all kinds of dry goods, fancy goods, dress goods, they spent it quite freely.

To show how freely they spent their money and how readily, I will state how I used to trade with them. I understood the language by that time, and I succeeded in gaining their confidence to such an extent that when they came from the mines with a bag of gold dust, they would bring it into the store, and tell me to weigh it and see how much there was of it. I would weigh out the dust, which might be worth anywhere from fifty to five or six hundred dollars, as the case might be. After weighing it, and telling the value of it, they would tell me to take it and put it away. I would put it into a box where I kept the gold I had on hand, and make a memorandum of the amount, and then they would commence calling for goods, one kind and another, whatever they wanted, and would make purchases of various articles for some time, I keeping a memorandum of what they took, and after they had selected a considerable quantity, they would ask me to count up and see how much the goods amounted to, and how much there was left of the gold dust unspent. So, after adding up the amount of their purchases, I would report the balance left to them, and they would commence calling for more goods, and go on buying, until after awhile they would ask me to count up again, and see how much they had left then, and so I would figure it up, and if there was still a balance left they would call for something more, and so on until the whole amount of gold was exhausted, when they would take the bundle of goods and go off satisfied. I had an old pair of scales I had rigged up for the occasion, and had correct weights, and I had got their confidence in regard to my dealings with them, and in regard to my weighing out the gold, and I was always careful to allow them for the exact amount of gold, and to give them a fair amount of goods for their money, of course charging a good profit, as goods were then high. I carried on business there through the years '48 and '49, and then finally sold out my whole business to another party and retired from it . . .[89]

After closing my business in San Jose I retired, and was married there in Feb'y '49 to an American lady.[90] I remained there resident while the government was organized and the legislature called in session at San Jose. The State Convention was held at Monterey, and the state

Josiah Belden and bride, San José, 1849
(Courtesy of Clyde Arbuckle)

Residence of Josiah Belden, San José, 1887

capitol was fixed at San Jose, and the legislature assembled
there in the winter of 49-50. San Jose was then incorpo-
rated under a new charter as a city, and in the Spring of
1850 I was elected mayor of the City under the new corpo-
ration, and I always regarded that as a very satisfactory
thing, inasmuch as San Jose was the place where I had been
arrested by the Mexican Government when I first came
to the country, as a kind of intruder, and been made a
prisoner, the people there thinking I wanted to create a
revolution, some nine years before.[91] It was simply an
instance showing how things worked round, and the change
which took place in the country. The American population had increased largely at the time the city was organized. About one quarter or one fifth of the population at
that time might have been the old Spanish settlers.

Among the leading families of the country, of the native
Californians, were Gen. Vallejo, Military Commander of
that part of the country; his brother Salvador Vallejo,
who was living there; another brother, Jose Jesus Vallejo,
who was living near San Jose; and another brother
Antonio. One of the sisters was married to Capt. John
B. Cooper, and another one to Jacob Leese of Sonoma.[92]
This was one of the most prominent families. One of Gen.
Vallejo's daughters was married to John B. Frisbie.[93]
Another of the most prominent men was J. B. Alvarado,
who was Governor from about '40 to '42; he had quite a
family of children. There was the family of Gen. Jose
Castro, Military Commandant at the time Alvarado was
Governor, in the southern and middle parts of the state.
These were three of the most prominent men in those
days, of the native Californians, very intelligent, ener-
getic, active, smart men, very gentlemanly in their deport-
ment and manner. There were other families somewhat

prominent,—the Pico family in San Jose, the Noriega
family, the Burrell family. Some of the Pico family lived
at San Jose. Don Pio Pico was governor, and his brother,
Andreas Pico, was prominent in the war.[94]

There were some little battles in California, one on the
Salinas Plains, where three or four were killed. Most
of the Mexican force was concentrated in the southern
country; the forces collected about Monterey marched
south. There was the battle of *La Mesa* on the table land
near Los Angeles, not very sanguinary, some few men
having been wounded, perhaps killed. There was a battalion known as the Fremont Battalion organized here in
California, composed partly of the men Fremont brought
out with him, and partly residents here, which marched
down south, expecting to join another force there composed in a great measure of men from the ship of war,
under command of Marvin, I think, which ship landed a
force of marines, who marched up to Los Angeles and had
a fight there, the battle of *La Mesa*. I think Fremont's
force did not reach there in time to participate in the fight.
I think that battle was subsequent to the battle of San Pasqu[a]l, which occurred east of San Diego somewhere.
There was quite a serious fight there between the forces of
Gen. Kearny, who had come across the Plains with a body
of troops, aided by some volunteers who had been stationed
at San Diego or somewhere down there, who united with
Kearny, on the one side, and the Californians under Andreas Pico, on the other. This battle of San Pasqu[a]l
resulted rather disastrously for the American forces, who
lost some sixteen killed, I think, while the Californians'
loss was but trifling.[95]

In the contest of Micheltoren[a] with the Californians
here at the time he was defeated and driven out, a con-

siderable number of Americans in the upper part of the country, around Sutter's Ft., who, I suppose, were in hopes of getting some favors from Micheltoren[a], in the way of grants of land, protection of rights, and other privileges, joined his forces, and Sutter himself sided with that party, and some of those also in his employ at the fort. These went down south with Micheltoreno, though Sutter himself I think did not go. A portion of the foreign population in the southern part of the state, about Los Angeles and neighborhood, joined the southern Californians under Pico. That brought one portion of the foreign residents in conflict with another portion. They were induced to favor one side or another, from local preferences, or some other interested motive. The foreign residents at the south were more under the influence of the Californians, were on more social and friendly terms with them, and therefore were inclined to side with them in the contest, while the foreigners up this way, especially round Sutter's Ft. and about the Sacramento Valley, joined with Micheltoren[a], because they considered it more for their interest to do so, to obtain land or something else they wanted. It was said that there was a kind of understanding between Sutter and Micheltoren[a], that if the Americans would assist him in his plans, he would favor them in obtaining grants of land in that part of the country, and it was said that he issued in advance, I think before they went south, a kind of provisional agreement that they should have the grants they had applied for, or something of that kind. Some of these grants were afterwards brought up for confirmation by the claimants, under what was understood as the provisional grant of Micheltoren[a], and I think one or two were confirmed, but others were rejected on that ground.[96]

Libby [Libbey] was captain of a Bark which came here to trade, a Boston vessel, and sometimes when he was ashore he was a pretty jolly sort of man, and liked to have his fun and frolic, and on one occasion he got into some trouble with the natives, and was shot, I think.[97]

The priests were thought to administer the affairs of the missions pretty well, but some of them were pretty loose in their morals, especially one at Santa Cruz, and another at Santa Clara. They were brothers, and each of them kept women. Some of them were pretty well educated. The priests here belonged to orders of friars, most to the order of Franciscans, and were mainly responsible, I suppose to the head of their order. They were perhaps subject to the head of the Church in Mexico, but of course, like all these Catholic priests, they acknowledged subordination to the Head of the Catholic Church, and to their bishops. The missions in their earlier days, before I came here, had been generally very thrifty and prosperous establishments, and accumulated considerable wealth, in the way of stock, &c.

When the first emigrants came here, they took the idea that the country was poorly adapted to agriculture, that it was too dry for general success in that line, and that it was mainly fit for stock raising; and the change of view in regard to this matter came on gradually, by Americans coming in here, and getting hold of land, and beginning to cultivate it. I dont think there was much attempt at agriculture here to any extent until after 1846. The new comers began to scatter round, and came into the Santa Clara Valley, and took up lands there, and began to cultivate them to some extent, and also to some extent on the other side of the bay, and round in various parts of the country. I dont think the raising of wheat for flour, for

the consumption of the people, was done to any extent
until along about '52 or '53. In 1849 a good deal of flour
was imported from Chil[e], and was somewhat scarce at
one time.

I think in the earlier years that I was here, from 1841
on, for perhaps ten or twelve years, the seasons were less
favorable for cultivation than they have been since. I
think there was more drouth. The winter of 1843, I think
it was, was the dryest season I have known since I have
been in the country. There was no record kept of the rain,
but it was an excessively dry year and I think the proportion of the dry seasons to the wet ones was greater from
1841 to '51 or '52 than it has been since. I think turning up
the soil to so large an extent has had a favorable effect
upon the rainfall.[98]

The only vehicles in use at first were primitive carts,
with solid block wheels, hauled by oxen, with yokes
lassoed on to their horns, and the tongue of the cart fast-
ened to that. Families, when they moved about from one
place to another, used these carts. They would have a
hide in the bottom; they also generally put a hide over the
top, and hides round the sides, and in that way made a
covered vehicle; they were very crude, without springs,
of course, the body of the cart lying right on the rough
wooden axel. The wheels were made of sections of trees
cut off, with a hole through the middle for the axel. The
families travelled in them, and they were also used for
carrying loads.

Of wild animals, there was the grizzly bear, very plenty
through the country, the panther or California lion, not
so plenty, the wolf, which the Californians called *lobo,*
I think, an animal larger and stronger and more ferocious
than the c[o]yote, a much smaller animal, very abundant

through the whole country. When I first went to San Jose, every night I heard the c[o]yotes howling all round the town. It was not very woody about San Jose, though there was some wood along the neighboring creeks. Deer were very plenty, and also antelope and elk, especially round the San Joaquin plains, and great numbers of wild horses in the Tulare plains. They were understood generally, I think, to be of the Andalusian breed of horses, introduced from Mexico probably, and originally from Spain. The originals were a fine breed of horses; amongst those they broke for use were fine saddle horses, never used for harness. There were great numbers of breeding mares kept through the country, all pretty much of the same stock, what were supposed to be the Andalusian breed, very excellent horses for their work, for managing cattle, for lassoing and driving cattle, capable of a good deal of endurance, even on very poor treatment. They were very rarely stabled, always ran out in the pastures. The rancheros generally had large numbers of horses, would keep two or three, as many as they needed for ordinary use, tied to the posts about the house generally, for a few days, and when they began to get a little thin from hard riding and want of feed, they would turn them out, and bring in some more. They were not left in stables, or groomed at all. Horses were very cheap at that time. You could buy a very good saddle horse for four or five dollars, broken to the saddle. They were very expert in handling and managing cattle. The horses who were well trained to it, seemed to understand it as well as a man could, catching cattle which were pretty wild, not many of them being kept about the ranches, but allowed to run about the plains; very few of them were kept for milch cows, and scarcely anything was done in the way of making butter and cheese; the milch cows were not very gentle, and when they were milked, their hind legs were always tied together to prevent them from kicking, and the head tied to a post. There was scarcely anything done toward improving the breed of the cattle, no new stock was introduced, and I suppose they had degenerated from breeding among themselves. Another disadvantage among the horses was, whenever they had an extra fine colt growing up, instead of keeping him for a stallion to improve their stock, they would have him castrated and broken to the saddle. The Californian's pride was in his horse and saddle and trappings.

They would sometimes have some little shrubbery and flowers perhaps a grapevine, about their houses, but very little in the way of adornment, very little cultivation of fruit except in the missions, where they had fruit orchards, and the population depended mainly upon these mission orchards for their supply.

In regard to the horses that the rancheros raised, they had large bands of breeding mares, and the horses multiplied to such an extent, that, in a season of drouth, when there was not sufficient feed for the cattle, at times they drove a lot of the mares, and perhaps some of the horses, over a precipice, to get rid of them, in order to save the feed for the cattle, which were of more value than the horses were, on account of their hides and tallow. They hardly ever cut any grass, had no barns, and in a dry time had nothing to rely upon. Occasionally a farmer might have a little pile of hay, but very rarely. So far as they fed their horses about the house, they used barley.

What grain they raised was threshed out by being put into a stack, and a corral was made, like a threshing floor of ancient times, an enclosure with a fence round it, generally circular, and the grain was spread over the ground, and a band of horses was turned in, and driven round over it, to tramp it out. They had the simplest kind of plough, about the same kind of plough that is used in Oriental countries today. The grain after being threshed out in this way was winnowed from the straw by choosing a time when there was a wind blowing, and taking the grain and throwing it up into the air, and the wind would blow the chaff away. They then washed it generally before they ground it, and made their flour in a mule mill, with two stones, one upon another, a bolt attached to the upper stone, and the stone revolved only as often as the mule went round, and so the operation of making flour was a very slow and tedious process.

The common people did not use much wheat flour, but they used corn, which they made into tortillas, a kind of flat cake, baked on iron. The beef was generally roasted upon an iron spit, and was cut in slits or strips, and cooked before an open fireplace. The principal food, what they lived on almost entirely, in fact, was beef, and *frijoles,* a reddish bean which they raised, and tortillas.[99] This was the common diet. You scarcely saw any potatoes or other vegetables in use. They raised peppers for seasoning their food, and were used in almost everything. They sometimes made a kind of stew, and when it was done, they introduced the peppers.

The ladies were quite fond of fine showy dresses, and generally dressed with very good taste too, as far as they had the means, and were rather pleasing in their dress, with not a great deal of jewelry, though rather fond of it. One almost universal article of dress among the ladies was called the *rebosa,* worn as a covering for the head and shoulders, a kind of scarf, used in place of a shawl, generally put over the head when going out, and hanging down over the shoulders. Some of these were very fine and costly, woven of silk, some were of cotton, some of linen, according to the condition of the wearer.

There were a good many Indians, besides those collected about the missions. The Indians of the coast were inferior to the Indians of the interior, inferior in physique and mental capacity to the Indians on the eastern side of the Rocky Mountains. Those that were civilized to some extent were very useful servants and laboring men for the rancheros and citizens; those about the missions were employed on the mission ranches, and rarely set up for themselves. Those that belonged to the missions were fed from the missions; they generally had little adobe houses round the mission church, and lived there, and were commonly docile and tractable.

Deer were so plenty here that some of the foreigners made a practice of hunting them for their skins, and selling them. In connection with the killing of deer for their skins, I will mention that a man by the name of Grove Cook, who came out with our party, when he first came into the country occupied himself for awhile with hunting deer and selling their skins, and he came in here to San Francisco.[100] There was a man who kept a little trading place here, by the name of Teal,[101] I think, and Cook went to his place to get a fitout when he was about starting out hunting, and the storekeeper furnished him with provisions and ammunition on credit, and was to take his pay in deer skins at 50 cents apiece, or whatever the price was. While he was supplying Cook with articles he wanted, he got talking with him in a friendly way, and explained to him his manner of doing business, saying he thought the best way was, when he got a customer to make all he could out of him, to skin him clean the first time, and never depend upon him for any future trade. Cook got his supplies, and went off hunting, and found young fawns pretty plenty, and shot them with the larger deer, as they came along, and before long had collected quite a large number of skins, large and small. He was to supply Teal with a certain number of skins, at so much apiece, to liquidate his debt to him, and took the number required into his store. Teal looked them over and said, "Here, Cook, a good many of these are fawns skins, quite small, and these wont pass for 50 cents apiece." Cook looked at him, and said, "I was to give you so many deer skins, at such a price?" "Yes, Sir," was the reply, "but I thought they were to be full sized skins." "They are all deer skins, aren't they?" asked Cook. "Yes, they are deer skins," answered the man. Said Cook, "Do you remember what you said to me about your mode of doing business: that your plan was to skin a man clean the first time you traded with him, and let him go? I thought I would take you at your word and act upon your plan. There are your skins, and we are all square."

Thomas O. Larkin, while doing business in Monterey, selling goods of course, received hides and tallow in pay mostly, instead of money, the hides at $2.00 apiece. The Spaniards used to bring the hides in to him, one, two, or three at a time, as the case might be. Larkin had a yard back of his store where he kept his hides. A man would bring a hide up to the store, and Larkin would tell him to take it back to the yard and throw it in, and would allow him his two dollars for it, in goods. Pretty soon another man would come in with his hide, and get his goods and go off, and so on, another and another. It was found out after a while that it was a practice among the Spaniards for one man to go and sell a hide to Larkin, and put it into the yard, and for another one to go and take it out, and sell it over again, and so on until it had been sold several times, and it was said that this trick was played on Larkin for some time.

The Spaniards were pretty sharp and shrewd. I remember buying a nice saddle horse of a man in Monterery, and I paid the man, and he went off. I tied the horse to a post some little distance from the store, and after awhile I looked out the door just in time to see an Indian riding off with my horse as fast as he could, and that was the last I saw of him. I presume the man who sold me the horse hired this Indian to go and get him, and deliver him out in the country somewhere, where he was waiting to receive him. They were up to all such little tricks.

They all had horses, however poor, and whenever they wanted to go anywhere, even only two or three hundred yards, they would ride. If the women rode by themselves, they rode astride, but the woman almost always rode sideways in front of the horse, and the man astride behind, on the same horse. When a young man and his girl were going anywhere, they would get on to his horse, and he would commonly take his hat off and put it on the girl's head, and tie a handkerchief round his own head, and in that way they would go riding around. That was rather a piece of gallantry on his part, and generally they would have a song to sing while they were riding. About the ranches in the towns, you would see little parties of young men and women going round in that way to a fandango or meeting. The young men would sometimes get on to their horses, one of them with a guitar, and ride round from place to place, or house to house, and most of them would be singing some tune they knew, one playing the guitar as an accompaniment. That was a very common thing. There was rarely a night in the village but there would be a dance somewhere.

There was rather a looseness among them in regard to their habits of chastity. The young girls were most generally pretty particular, but among the commoner class of married women there was a looseness in this respect; not remarkably so, but it was generally understood that they were less severe than the American people in this respect. The women occupied themselves with the care of their families and sewing, generally made their own clothing, and the common class of clothing for their husbands, were generally domestic, but spent considerable time in visiting, going to parties, dances, &c. There was one good feature about the female portion of the community; they were generally very clean in their habits and about their houses, even if they had a house with only a dirt floor. They used to wash a good deal out of doors generally going to some spring or creek in the neighborhood, and seldom did much washing in the house.

The ship "Brooklyn" arrived here in 1846, soon after the raising of the American flag, with a party of Mormons, under Sam Brannan. They came from New York, and were gathered mainly from New York and the Eastern states, I think. They formed an association there, and chartered the vessel and fitted her out for the voyage, and loaded her with such supplies as they thought they would need in forming a new settlement, provisions, agricultural implements, arms, ammunition, &c. They landed in San Francisco, and it was generally understood that they came here with the intention of taking possession of the place, and driving out the Mexican authorities; and the plan was, I think, for another party to come across the plains, and form a connection here somewhere in the country with those who came by ship, and with this force set up an

independent government here, and make themselves strong
enough to expel those in power here, and build up a Mormon government here, and hold the country. It was said
that they brought an independent flag ready made, and
intended to be hoisted here. I think there were about 130
of them altogether, men, women and children, perhaps
150. When they got here they landed, and most of them
located here, and a few went to other parts of the country.
But fortunately for the country, I presume, and perhaps
in the end for them, they arrived just a little too late, the
place having been taken possession of by the American
government. It was thought they were very much disap-
pointed when they came into the harbor, and found the
American flag flying here. They were completely non-
plused, as it overturned all their calculations and plans.
I dont think there was any polygamy amongst that party
which landed here. Most of them proved to be industrious
and enterprising working business people, and contributed
considerably towards developing the resources of the state
and building up the town, acquired property here, especially Brannan, a very active, energetic man, but rather erratic.
They used to say that he attempted to exercise pretty abso-
lute control over the people who came out with him, under
the church government, and that he got a lot of them to
go to work mining, and used to supply them with goods,
and that they worked there awhile under this arrangement; at first he undertook to enforce the Mormon law of
demanding one tenth of all they acquired, for the church,
and it was said they paid it for awhile; but finally they
came to the conclusion that they would not pay him one
tenth of their gold any longer, and they came into his
store and told him they were not going to pay him any
such tithe any longer. "You have come to that conclusion,

have you?" asked Brannan. "Yes," was the reply. "Well," said he, "All I can say is you were damned fools to have paid it as long as you have." Some of them went off to Salt Lake; others scattered through the country, and probably lost their connection with the church.[102]

Footnotes to Statement

1 Belden's version here of his youth conflicts with two statements he previously gave on the subject. Shuck, p. 919; Phelps, I, 246, present a more accurate and detailed appraisal which has been utilized in the brief biographical sketch given in the Introduction. *DAB,* II, 145, places his birth in Cromwell, Connecticut, failing to note that the community's name had been changed from Upper Middletown.

2 Belden's references are to the books of James Fennimore Cooper and to Washington Irving's, *Astoria, or Anecdotes of an Enterprise Beyond the Rocky Mountains* (Philadelphia, 1836).

3 As pointed out in the Introduction, the Bartleson party did have some information to guide them.

4 Belden's three traveling companions were David W. Chandler, Henry L. Brolaski, and George Shotwell. Shotwell never reached California. As John Bidwell relates, he accidentally shot himself, June 13, "while in the act of taking a gun out of the wagon, drew it, with the muzzle towards him in such a manner that it went off and shot him near the heart—he lived about an hour and died in full possession of his senses. His good behavior had secured him the respect and good will of all the company, he had resided some 8 or 9 months on or near the Nodaway River, Platte purchase Missouri prior to his starting on this expedition; but he said his mother lived in Laurel County, Kentucky, and was much opposed to his coming into the West—he was buried in the most decent manner our circumstances would admit of after which a funeral sermon was preached by Mr. Williams." *Journey,* p. 7 (although on p. 1, Bidwell incorrectly lists the name as James Shotwell). *Williams Narrative,* p. 225, states that the burial took place 8 miles below

Ash Creek or Ash Hollow on the south fork of the Platte. Williams gives the date as June 20, but Bidwell's would appear to be the more accurate; affirmed by *John Diary.*

Chandler, having resided in California until 1847, and having been employed by Vioget for a number of those California years, tried Hawaii in an effort to get ahead, but returned to the coast in 1848. He is reported as having died in California. Bancroft, II, 757; Vioget to Sutter, February 18, 1842. *Six French Letters* [:] *Captain John Augustus Sutter to Jean Jacques Vioget, 1842-1843,* p. 150. Bidwell, *Journey,* p. 1, lists J. W. Chandler.

Brolaski did not tarry long in California. He moved to Monterey in 1842. From there he sailed to Callao, probably residing there for several years. By 1848, he was back in St. Louis, anxious to return west. Infected with gold-fever, he did return in 1849. Bancroft, II, 731; *Larkin Papers,* II, 170; *Missouri Republican,* July 7, 1849; *Argonauts of California,* p. 402. Bidwell, *Journey,* p. 1, lists H. S. Brolaske.

5 The party sporadically assembled two miles west of the Kansas River by May 16. On the 18th, rules and regulations for the trek west were adopted. *Ibid.,* p. 2. *John Diary* notes that the company camped at Wakaroatia Creek.

6 Thomas Fitzpatrick, long established as a *mountain man,* was employed as guide for the Jesuit missionary party. For a roster of this party's membership, consult pp. 126-136.

7 Belden's listing of the members of the party is inaccurate. See pp. 126-136 for the full membership.

Other then a number of omissions, Belden has three mistakes in his list. There was no Bartlett; perhaps Belden meant William Belty. Likewise, there is no listing of James Littlejohn. This should have been James John who was nicknamed "Jimmy John." Bidwell, *Echoes,* p. 39. The reference to Pfeiffer is undoubtedly meant to be Augustus Fifer or Pfeifer.

8 For a discussion of the rosters of the parties, see pp. 126-136.

9 The rules and regulations were not adopted until May 18th. Only once during the trek west were the rules decisively enforced. Bidwell, *Journey,* p. 6, notes under date of June 10, near the south fork of the Platte: "Through the remissness of the sentinels, the guard last night was nearly vacant; and as this was consid-

ered dangerous ground on account of the warlike Pawnees, Chi-
ennes [Cheyennes] &c. a Court Martial was called to force those
to their duty on guard, who were so negligent & remiss."

10 Belden is mistaken. Bidwell lists five women and an unstated
number of children in the party. There were two Mrs. Kelseys:
Mrs. Benjamin and Mrs. Samuel Kelsey. In addition, there
was the widow, Mrs. Gray (probably a sister of the latter Mrs.
Kelsey) and Mrs. Richard Williams and daughter. Miss Williams
married Isaac Kelsey on the trail, June 1. Mrs. Gray took
Richard Fillan [Phelan, according to Dale L. Morgan] (whom
Bidwell calls Cocrum, and *John Diary* calls Cockrel) as her
husband after he joined the party at Fort Laramie, July 23.
The Rev. Williams performed the first marriage and Fr. De
Smet, the second. Bidwell, *Journey,* pp. 4, 12; *Williams Narra-
tive,* pp. 221-222; *John Diary.*

11 Bidwell, *Journey,* p. 2, states that his party had 15 wagons and
the missionaries had 4 carts and a small wagon. *Williams Narrative,* p. 220, has 20 wagons in the party. Later, Bidwell, *Narrative,* p. 16, lists the missionary party with 5 or 6 "Red River"
carts drawn by two mules each. The Bartleson party's wagons
were drawn by mules, some by oxen.

Nicholas Dawson kept a detailed travel chronology of the trek
west. (*MS,* Bancroft Library. Hereafter cited *Dawson Chronology.* Copy courtesy of Dale L. Morgan.) I have used his dates
and place designations to articulate Belden's overland account
of the trip.

12 This was Nicholas Dawson, later renowned because of this incident as "Cheyenne" Dawson. The encounter took place along
the banks of the Platte, June 4th. *Williams Narrative,* pp. 222-
223, describes it: "On Friday evening the company had a ter-
rible alarm. One of our hunters who was in the rear, was robbed
of all he had by the Indians. They struck him with their ram-
rods, and he ran from them. Soon a war party of the Sioux
Indians appeared in view. We soon collected together in order
to battle, to be ready in case of an attack. The Indians stood
awhile and looked at us, and probably thinking that 'the better
part of valor is discretion,' they soon showed signs of peace.
Captain Fitzpatrick then went to them, and talked with them,

for he was acquainted with them. They then gave back all that they had taken from the young man, and our men gave them some tobacco, and they smoked the pipe of peace." Also, *Dawson Narrative*, pp. 11-12; *De Smet Letters*, I, 311-312; Bidwell, *Journey*, p. 4.

13 This incident took place near the Platte. Fitzpatrick and John Gray were able to handle the situation diplomatically. LeRoy R. Hafen and W[illiam] H. Ghent, *Broken Hand, The Life of Thomas Fitzpatrick*, pp. 131-132.

14 The trapper involved was Henry Fraeb, an old friend and trail companion of Fitzpatrick. Fraeb and his party met up with the company on the Green River, July 23. The incident alluded to by Belden took place a month after the parties split. Fraeb, with several of his companions, was slain in a fight with the Cheyenne and Sioux near the Colorado-Wyoming boundaries at a place later known as Battle Creek. *Williams Narrative*, p. 230; LeRoy R. Hafen, "Fraeb's Last Fight and How Battle Creek Got Its Name," *Colorado Magazine*, VII (1930), 97-101; Nolie Mumey, *The Life of Jim Baker*, pp. 22-23. *John Diary* gives the date as the 22nd, noting that the hunter's party consisted of 60 men. The *Dawson Chronology* notes that the party was traveling along the Green River, July 23-25, and on the 24th was encamped.

Charles Flügge, who joined the Oregon splinter party, later deciding to travel south from there to California, reached Sutter's Fort, December 27, 1841. (Bancroft, III, 741, believes Flügge came by land down from Oregon. The advanced season of the year would make this seem unlikely. Mayhap he came by the coastal bark, the *Columbia*.) Nevertheless, it was he who conveyed the news of Fraeb's death to his former trail companions. He reported that Fraeb and "1 of his men were killed by Chienne [Cheyenne] Indians 2 or 3 days after we had left [them on the trail]." Bidwell, *Journey*, p. 30. This version conflicts with several other reports. See Hafen's article cited above, pp. 97-101.

15 The date of this division, August 11, is given by Bidwell, *Journey*, p. 14; the place, Soda Springs in Idaho. *Dawson Chronology* enters the date as August 10. For a full discussion of how the party split, consult pp. 126-136.

Belden's memory here is faulty. Four of the California bound company traveled to Fort Hall with Fitzpatrick to glean any additional information they could about the route west. About ten days later the four men returned to join the Bartleson party which had in the meantime traveled some 100 miles toward Salt Lake. They brought information that the route west should be south of that Lake, with caution not to go too far south since they would hit an arid wasteland. Caution was also needed so as not to go too far north, for there the party might end up in a maze of rugged canyons. Bidwell, *Echoes,* pp. 38-39, 42.

16 Bancroft, IV, 270, fixes the remaining number at "thirty-two men—with one woman and child, the wife and daughter of Benjamin Kelsey."

17 Bartleson and Charles Hopper were the scouts. According to Bidwell, *Journey,* p. 18, they left the company on August 29, rejoining them September 9, after having located a branch of St. Mary's River. *Dawson Chronology* records the arrival at a "Good spring" on August 27. His dates indicate the party remained there at least through September 4, moving on the 5th.

18 Bartleson and eight others struck out on their own, October 7, but rejoined the caravan October 16. Bidwell, *Journey,* p. 23.

19 Bidwell records that four or five of the party went scouting on October 16. *Ibid.,* p. 23.

20 Bidwell entered under date of September 23, the fact that while still looking for St. Mary's River, they were able to catch a few trout to supplant a growingly dangerous lack of food. But under date of November 1, only four days march away from their objective, Dr. Marsh's rancho, game was killed along with fowl: 13 deer and antelopes were brought into camp for the half-starved emigrees. Writing on this occasion, Bidwell remarked: "My breakfast, this morning, formed a striking contrast with that of yesterday which was the lights [lungs] of a wolf." *Ibid.,* pp. 21, 28.

21 Andrew Kelsey and Thomas Jones had left the party in October 24, to forge ahead. It was they who returned to the company on November 4, with Marsh's gift of supplies. *Ibid.,* pp. 26, 28.

22 George D. Lyman, *John Marsh, Pioneer,* has rendered a tolerable biography. Suffice it to state here that Marsh had journeyed to California in 1836 via the southern route from Santa Fé,

arriving in early January. After several years of medical practice in the Los Angeles area, based on his Harvard B.A., he traveled rather extensively in the northern parts of the state. By 1839, he obtained the Los Médanos rancho at the foot of Mt. Diablo. He must be considered as a contributory cause to the 1841 emigration since he wrote a number of letters extolling the virtues of California, urging emigrants to come west. Bidwell, however, was far from impressed with Marsh's hospitality and surroundings. For two views on this matter, Bancroft, IV, 273-274, and *notes;* Caughey, p. 213.

23 *Dawson Narrative,* p. 27, states that a number of the party went to the Stanislaus River first, among them Kelsey and Bidwell. Bidwell, *Echoes,* pp. 69-70, later recollects that he visited Don José Amador on his Livermore ranch, while others went south of Marsh's rancho. Bidwell was in San José by November 18, because on that date Mariano Vallejo issued him a passport. *John Bidwell Papers,* CSL.

24 Under date of November 6, Bidwell, *Narrative,* p. 74, and in his *Journey,* p. 29, notes that fifteen of the company started for San José to "seek employment." In crossing Livermore Ranch, Belden's San José bound party must have run across the small settlement on that property. Under November 10, Bidwell reports that he visited that ranch, some twenty miles from Marsh's, where he found "5 or 6 Spanish families." *Ibid.,* p. 30.

On November 5, Marsh notified Antonio María Sunol, the Sub-Prefect of his district, of the arrival of 31 men, listing them by name. *Vallejo MSS,* X, 300, Bancroft Library. James John had forged ahead on his own. He left the company October 20 and safely made Sutter's Fort. Bidwell, *Journey,* pp. 25-26.

John A. Sutter, writing to Mariano Vallejo, September 19, 1841, reported: "A strong body of American farmers are coming here, a young man of the party got lost since 10 Days, nearly starved to death and on foot [James John]; he don't know which Direction the party took. I believe they will come about the Direction of the Pueblo [San José]."

In a subsequent letter, Sutter wrote to Jacob P. Leese, November 8, 1841: ". . . an other party is close by from Missouri—one of the party arrived here, some of my friends and acquaintances are among them, they are about forty or fifty men of Respectability and Property. They came in the intention to settle here." Cited letters in *Vallejo MSS*, X, 282, 332, Bancroft Library; copies in *John A. Sutter Collection*, CSL.

25 This was the Palo rancho of Joaquín Higuera. Shuck, p. 290. Belden, writing to his sister from Monterey, December 21, 1841, makes no mention of this event; rather he implies the party went directly to San José where they were arrested.

26 In another account, Belden states they were arrested two miles from the pueblo. His traveling companions included Henry L. Brolaski, Charles Weber, Grove Cook, Michael Nye, and James Springer. Bidwell, *Echoes*, p. 71; Hall, p. 135; Shuck, p. 921.

27 Their total confinement lasted only six days. The reason for the confinement, due to the abortive foreign affair led by Isaac Graham in 1840, is described in Bancroft, IV, 274-275.

28 James Alexander Forbes had been a resident of the San José area from 1836. In 1842 he was made British vice-consul. Bancroft, IV, 274-275, makes no mention of Forbes acting in the capacity described by Belden, but in his "Pioneer Register," III, 743, states that he acted as bondsman for some of the Bartleson party. Marsh was called to San José for consultation with the Mexican authorities and vouched for the peaceful intentions of the emigrants.

Belden and Brolaski made for Santa Cruz, then Monterey. Shuck, p. 923.

29 Testaments to the dryness of the 1841 season are found in Bidwell, *Journey*, pp. 28, 34-36; *Dawson Narrative*, p. 30, and *Niles' Register*, May 22, October 16, 1841.

30 Bidwell, *Journey*, p. 44, fixes San José's population at 300 in 1841.

31 For a short summary of California government under Mexico, see Paul Mason, "Constitutional History of California," *Constitution of the State of California . . . 1957*, pp. 243-273.

32 Juan Bautista Alvarado was governor of California, 1839-1841. He had been revolutionary governor from December 7, 1836 to July 9, 1837. José Castro had been appointed captain of the Monterey garrison in 1839. Mariano Guadalupe Vallejo rose in the military service to the rank of captain and colonel of *defens-*

ores. In 1839 he was made *ayudante militar* by the Mexican government.

33 The reference here is to the native California uprising against Governor Mariano Chico's successor, Nicholas Gutierrez, in 1836 led by Juan Batista Alvarado. In the execution of the revolt, a number of Americans in and around the San Francisco Bay area supported Alvarado.

34 Chief among the Americans arrested by Alvarado was Isaac Graham, one of his allies in the 1836 revolt. For a vivid, but prejudiced treatment of this event, see T[homas] J. Farnham, *The Early Days of California*, p. 52, *et seq.*, wherein he lists the number of men sent to prison at 41 (p. 112). Other views of the affair are given in Larkin's letter to James G. Bennett, February 10, 1843. *Larkin Papers,* II, 7-9, and as reported in *Niles' Register,* August 15, 1840. It was this occurrence that caused trouble for Belden and his companions when they reached San José and were arrested.

   April 20, 1844, in writing to the Secretary of State, Larkin expostulated: "I am of the opinion that Cal[i]fornia had no just cause for the arresting and shipping of these men [in 1840]." *Larkin Papers,* II, 101. Benjamin D. Wilson, dictating his memoirs for H. H. Bancroft in 1877, took a very dim view of Graham's character and behavior. *MS,* Bancroft Library; copy, *Shorb Papers,* HEH.

35 On his return from San Blas, having been interned there in 1840, Graham in company with Henry Naile procured the Rancho Sayante near Santa Cruz. There they built a saw mill. Naile had arrived in California in 1836 from New Mexico. He died, April, 1846, at the hands of James Williams. *Dawson Narrative,* p. 37, notes that the only saw-mill in California was located at Santa Cruz and was owned by Graham, Naile, and Joseph Majors.

36 It can only be surmised that the Ferguson here referred to is Daniel Ferguson, an Irishman, who came to California from New Mexico. He married Carman Ruíz. His name appears as early as 1832 in the Monterey area, and crops up in the *Larkin Papers* for the years 1839-1840.

37 Belden is here mistaken. His reference should be to Joseph L. Majors who came to California from New Mexico, and who was

an old friend of Graham's. In 1839 he was naturalized, taking the name of Juan José Crisóstomo. In 1841 he acquired land grants to the San Augustin and Sayante ranchos, disposing of the latter to Isaac Graham. He married María de los Angeles Castro by whom he had 19 children. He died at Santa Cruz, 1869.

William Ware arrived from New Mexico [?] probably in 1832 and settled in the Santa Cruz area. He worked as a distiller, tanner, and lumberman, eventually becoming a farmer. He died in 1868.

38 A fandango is a dance form. When used in the plural, it denotes a social dance.

39 Belden means an *arroba,* a 25 lb. measure of tallow.

40 The custom house at Monterey was established in 1842 and was built by Larkin. Letter to Andrew Johnstone, [June 13, 1843]. *Larkin Papers,* II, 20.

41 Viniculture in California was fathered from the Missions. Around 1770 the first vines were planted at San Diego and spread accordingly as the Missions grew. By the 1830's pioneer vineyards had been planted in Sonoma County. The bulk of the production was wine; only about one-fourth of each crop was turned into "aguardiente." This item, however, constituted an important ingredient in California mercantile activities. Vincent P. Carosso, *The California Wine Industry, 1830-1896,* pp. 2-9; Nicholas Den to Larkin, January 16, 1842. *Larkin Papers,* I, 156.

By 1842, a tax of $10.00 a barrel was levied on foreign liquor being imported into California. Belden to Larkin, May 4, 1842. *Ibid.,* p. 218.

42 Larkin reported to the Secretary of State, April 16, 1844: "Most of the U.S. Vessells have a hide house in San Diego, where they always keep a Mate & some men to cure their hides as they collect them from different Ports in California." *Ibid.,* II, 96. Adele Ogden, "Boston Hide Droghers Along California Shores," *CHSQ,* VIII, (1929), 289-305, offers a condensed statement on the early hide and tallow trade.

43 Wheat was, indeed, an important commodity for the Russians. Alpheus B. Thompson to Larkin, October, 13, 18, 1845. *Larkin Papers,* IV, 22, 47-48; Capt. T. C. Everett to Howard, October 19, 1845. *W.D.M. Howard Papers,* CHS.

44 Sutter received eleven square leagues (48,818 acres) on June 18, 1841, and soon after negotiated the Russian Fort Ross purchase. James P. Zollinger, *Sutter . . .*, p. 103.

Belden's appraisal of Sutter, given in his dictation manuscript on page 55 (which is here transposed), reads:

"Sutter was considered a very generous, hospitable, good man, and he had the confidence of the authorities, and they gave him large grants of land, and encouraged him to settle and build up an establishment where he was located."

45 California's marvelous wheat production was praised by Bidwell, *Journey*, p. 33, and found national attention in *Niles' Register*, September 11, 1841, which claimed it to be a hardy and bountiful grower.

46 Chiles, Nye, and Rickman headed for the Sacramento fort, two of them soon after moving on to Monterey. Later, Chiles joined Bartleson, Cook, and Hopper on the San Joaquin for the winter. Sutter to Larkin, January 26, 1842. *Larkin Papers*, I, 159; *Hopper Narrative*, Bancroft Library.

47 Larkin employed Belden in December, 1841. On February 3, 1842, he sent Belden to Santa Cruz as his agent, entrusting him with an inventory of goods amounting to $2,188.00. His employment proved highly successful. Writing to Larkin, March 28, Belden reported that he had sold some $1,250.00 of the inventory; had taken in $40.00 in cash; 100 hides with 20 more due; 11,500 feet of lumber, and another 40,00 feet due; and some 4,000 shingles. By April 5th, plans were being made to move the lumber for transfer to Captain John Paty's ship. Letters from Belden to Larkin under above cited dates, *Larkin Papers*, I, 161-163, 182-184, 187-188.

48 Belden's memory is incorrect here. In examining the lumber inventories he received at Santa Cruz, Graham and his partner's name do not appear. Since they owned a saw-mill, it is more likely that the lumber-jacks, the important ones being Samuel Thompson and James Rogers, contracted independently with Graham and Naile for their services and sold the finished products directly to Belden. Belden to Larkin, March 28, April 5 and 13, 1842. *Ibid.*, pp. 183, 187-188, 191-192.

49 Since Belden's major shipment of hides (some 200) took place

in mid-July, the incident mentioned in his narration might well be dated at this time. Belden to Larkin, July 20, 1842. *Ibid.,* p. 250.

50 Belden reported the news to Larkin, May 29, 1842. In his account of the theft, he placed the entire blame on "the priest" and comments on the handkerchiefs as an item of proof. The value of goods stolen was fixed at $150.00 in a report dated December 30, 1842. *Ibid.,* pp. 228, 350.

In 1833, Fr. Antonio Suárez del Réal was appointed priest to the Santa Cruz Mission. He served in that capacity until 1843, at which time the Mission was abandoned. His tenure there was plagued, after the secularization of the Missions, with extreme poverty and privation. He could have hardly afforded a "house-keeper." Writing to Fr. Vice-Comisario, Lorenzo Quíjas, December 7, 1843, just prior to the abandonment of Santa Cruz, Fr. Antonio graphically expressed the plight of his situation and commented on the widespread thefts by the Indians. His established reputation with his order, the Franciscans, leads one to suspect that Belden's store was probably robbed by one of the priest's local flock who were trying either to do him a service or else were trying to ingratiate themselves with their pastor. Fr. Zephyrin [Charles A.] Engelhardt, *The Mission and Missionaries of California,* III, 452; IV, 261, 297-298, 394.

Also, see Belden's letter to his sister from Santa Cruz, March 21, 1842, *post.*

51 The fire took place during the last week in May, 1843. So provoked was Larkin on his loss that he issued a public notice calling for the discovery and exposure of the culprits. If this failed, he threatened to terminate his operations in the Santa Cruz area; a threat he carried out. Belden returned to Monterey and clerked for Larkin during the remainder of 1843. Public Notice, June 1, 1843. *Larkin Papers,* II, 18; Belden to his sister, June 15, 1845. In a later autobiographical memoir, Belden states that the loss from the lumber fire totaled $6,000. Shuck, p. 924.

52 The date of this seizure was October 19, 1842. For full details, Robert G. Cleland, *A History of California . . .,* pp. 148-150; Bancroft, IV, 298-329. *Niles' Register,* January 28, February 11, 1843, gave extensive accounts of this American "fiasco."

53 This would be Nicholas "Cheyenne" Dawson. After a brief stay in Santa Cruz, Dawson went south to Santa Barbara. *Dawson Narrative,* p. 37, *et seq.*

54 William Thompson's real name was William Buckle. He was brother to Samuel Buckle (or Thompson). Very little is known about William in contrast to Samuel (see Bancroft, II, 734-735). However, the two brothers were actively engaged as lumber-jacks ("sawyers" as Belden calls them) in the Santa Cruz area by 1842. Belden to Larkin, April 5, 13, 1842. *Larkin Papers,* I, 187-188, 192.

55 The men in the hills referred to here by Belden are listed in his reports to Larkin as William Brander, George Chapel, Elijah Ness, James Rogers, William Trevathan, William Ware, Alvin Wilson, Francis Young, all lumber-jacks.

Michael Lodge was living at Monterey by 1829. He married Martina Castro. By 1837 he owned a ranch near Santa Cruz that had a beach frontage. Belden utilized "Lodge's beach" as the "wharf" for his lumber and hide shipments. Lodge had two daughters. One of them married Thomas Fallon. Although the marriage had five children, it ended in divorce.

56 José de Jesús Vallejo, born in 1798, was active in military and political life of Mexican California. He was military commander at San José at the time of Belden's imprisonment.

57 Bancroft, IV, 350-367, treats Micheltorena's early governorship, noting that he did receive support from such men as Sutter, Bidwell, and Larkin. The revolution is discussed in the same volume, pp. 455-517. The battle of "Canuga" mentioned by Belden is the battle which took place at Cahuenga, or the Alamo as some refer to it, February 20-21, 1845. For Sutter's and other American participation, *The Diary of Johann August Sutter,* pp. 19-27. For more first-hand details, Larkin to Parrott & Co., January 21; to Secretary of State, January 25, 1845. *Larkin Papers,* III, 20-21, 22-24.

58 Bancroft, IV, 515-516, and *notes,* discusses this aspect of the revolt. Also, see Larkin to John C. Calhoun, March 22, 1845. *Larkin Papers,* III, 79-82.

59 Larkin to Micheltorena; John C. Jones to Larkin, March 21, 1845. *Ibid.,* pp. 74-77.

60 The land grant given to Belden was the Barranca Colorado rancho in the upper Sacramento Valley near present-day Red Bluff. It comprised 21,000 acres, although Belden in his narrative refers to 18,000 acres. For the first figure, see Belden's letter to his sister, June 15, 1845, *post.*

Larkin, writing to Moses Y. Beach, May 28, 1845, pointed out the ease with which Mexican citizenship could be acquired. All an applicant had to do was to have two witnesses vouch that he was a "worthy person," then pay the fee of $8. Once a Mexican, payment of an $18 fee to the Governor's Secretary would obtain a grant of any vacant lands not over eleven square leagues in size. *Larkin Papers,* III, 202.

The following account describes the background of the land Belden acquired: "The land on the west bank of the Feather river, from Table mountain to Sutter's line, was originally granted to Flugge, who failed to make the required settlement in time, and it was denounced by two brothers named Fernandez, who obtained a grant thereto, which is perfectly valid. . . . The grant is for 4 leagues, or 17,754.73 acres, being 1 league in breadth and 4 in length along the river. Mr. Joshua [Josiah] Belden, of San Jose, owns two-thirds of this claim, and the brothers the remaining one-third." A. Vandorn to Col. John C. Hays, July 15, 1855, printed in the Sacramento *Daily Democratic State Journal,* October 27, 1855 (from the Stockton *Argus*). This is perhaps a more accurate account of Belden's rancho.

61 The reference to Hartnell and Cooper could mean only William Hartnell and John Bautista Roger Cooper. Susanna B. Dakin had contributed a biography of the former, *The Lives of William Hartnell.* There is no extant biography on Cooper. This is partly due to the fact that the bulk of the manuscripts dealing with his life are still in private hands.

62 Traveling the "Old Mexican Trail" via the Wasatch Mountains and the Little Salt Lake, this party of around 23 Americans left the western most part of New Mexico, at a place called "Abiquiú," in the first week of September, 1841. They arrived at Cucamonga, December 12, 1841. Arthur Woodward, (ed.), "Benjamin David Wilson's Observations on Early Days in California and New Mexico," *Annual Publications* of the Historical Society

of Southern California, XVI (1934), 86, 136; H. D. Barrows, "Don David W. Alexander," *ibid.,* IV (1897), 43. Wilson dates the party's arrival in November, but Alexander, another party member, gives the more approximate date.

Bancroft, IV, 278, *note,* gives the list of the members of the Workman-Rowland party. The list given here by Belden omits the names of Frank Bedibey, James Doke, Jacob Frankfort, Frank Gwinn, L. (or J. H.) Lyman, Daniel Sexton, Michael White. Belden misspells Tibeau and mistakenly has William C. Moon included. Bancroft does not include Pickman in his list. This would seem correct after examining the San Francisco *Herald,* June 15, 1856.

63 It is difficult to ascertain with precision all the members in the Bartleson party who returned east or left California. Nine of the Workman-Rowland party left, or at least so Bancroft states.

64 Albert G. Toomes after his California arrival, moved north. In partnership with R. H. Thomes he established a carpentry and building business in San Francisco, moving to Monterey in 1843. After marrying María Isabel Lorenzana in 1844, he was naturalized and received the Río de los Molinos rancho in Tehama County. Although the rancho was utilized, he did not settle on it until 1849. He died in 1873, being survived by his widow of five years.

65 Overland emigrations to California in 1843 were smaller than anticipated. Lansford W. Hastings, after captaining a party of 160 to Oregon, was able to bring some 36 or 38 of that group to California. Starting out from Oregon toward the end of May, they arrived opposite Sutter's Fort on or about July 10th.

The second 1843 party was organized and led by Joseph B. Chiles, an original member of the 1841 emigration, who had returned east. At Fort Laramie the party engaged Joseph R. Walker as guide for the rest of the trip west. As to the number in the Chiles-Walker party, Bancroft guesses no more than 50.

However, only one of the four men listed by Belden is to be found among the pioneers of 1843. This would be Major Samuel J. Hensley (who had been a pledged member of the 1841 emigration society, but withdrew!) whose name Belden spells Hixley. Jacob R. Snyder and William Blackburn came in the Swasey-Todd party of 1845. As to Major Rich, this could have been the William Rich who came in 1841.

66 The emigrants of 1844 came in two parties, one of 36 persons from Oregon, the other, the Stevens-Murphy party. A few under 100 new arrivals are accounted for that year.

Belden, however, fails to take note of the 1845 arrival of five emigrant groups, by far the largest number of newcomers up to that date, some 250 persons.

1846 pioneer arrivals are fixed at around 1,000 by Bancroft. In arriving at that figure, Bancroft includes those men who came to California in the military service at the beginning of the Mexican War.

67 Belden's recollections here are accurate. For an excellent first-hand report of the Bear Flag Revolt, see James Henry Gleason's letter to William Paty, Monterey, June 18, 1846. Duncan Gleason, (ed.), "James Henry Gleason: Pioneer Journal and Letters, 1841-1856," Historical Society of Southern California *Quarterly,* XXXI (1949), 23-24. Hereafter cited *Gleason Letters.* John A. Hawgood, "John C. Frémont and the Bear Flag Revolution," *University of Birmingham Historical Journal,* VII (1959), 80-100, presents a reappraisal of this event.

68 Bancroft in his "Pioneer Register" does not indicate Ide as a Mormon. Writing in volume V, 158, *note,* Bancroft discusses this matter and holds to the contrary.

69 Belden is inaccurate here. His reference is to the attempt on the part of Fowler (whose first name Bancroft never establishes) and Thomas Cowie to obtain some gunpowder. They were slain by Californians, but the exact circumstances remain clouded. *Ibid.,* p. 161.

James Gleason, writing to R. C. Wyllie from Monterey, July 3, 1846, stated: "It is reported here that the Californians took two foreigners prisoners on the road and barbarously murdered them. And in return the American party shot three Californians, couriers from Jose Antonio Carrillo to General Castro. One of them was Manuel Castro, brother-in-law to the General." *Gleason Letters,* p. 27.

70 A party of seventeen or eighteen volunteers were dispatched from Sonoma to rescue the prisoner on June 23. The following morning

the prisoners made contact with the retreating Californians and took three or four prisoners. Later in the same day, June 24, a larger force of Californians was encountered and after a brief skirmish they retreated. The day was carried by the Bear Flag forces.

71 Belden is close to the actual facts.

72 For Frémont's activities, which Belden here relates fairly accurately, Bancroft, V, 1-23.

73 Frémont was brought to trial.

74 William M. Gwin received the six-year term, Frémont, the two-year term.

75 Belden's reference here is to the unsuccessful scheme by an Irish priest, Eugene McNamara, to colonize indigent Irishmen in California to confound the United States.

76 *H.M.S. Collingwood,* under the command of Admiral Sir George Seymour on the eve of the United States' declaration of war against Mexico, was closely watching the activities of Commodore Sloat's fleet in Mazatlán harbor. By deceptive tactics, Sloat evaded the British and made for California. Eight days later, the *Collingwood* appeared—too late to assert British claims to California. *Davis Recollections,* pp. 267-268. The best treatment for the background of this incident, see Ephraim D. Adams, "British Interests in California," *American Historical Review,* XIV (1909), 744-763.

77 John Parrott, United States consul at Mazatlan, had engaged in coastal trade for several years. In 1845, the English brig, *Star of the West,* Captain William Atherton, carrying a cargo valued at $120,000 consigned to Parrott, went aground, July 27, 1845, at Punta de los Lobos in Carmel Bay. One-half to two-thirds of her cargo was saved since they had been carefully packed in "waterproof wrapping." The salvaged goods were admitted duty free since the custom officials labeled them "damaged goods." Captain J. B. R. Cooper of Monterey secured a goodly portion of the wreck's goods. *Davis Recollections,* pp. 161-162. Bancroft, IV, 568, *note,* states to the contrary, that ". . . all that was saved was sold to Belden and others for $3,000." Larkin to James Watson, July 31, 1845, describes the event. Subsequently, the question of salvage produced considerable controversy. *Larkin Papers,* III,

288, 300, 321-325; John A. Swan, "Wreck of the Schooner, *Star of the West*, 1845," *MS*, Bancroft Library; Parrott to William A. Leidesdorff, August 15, 1845. *Leidesdorff Papers*, HEH.

One thing undoubtedly resulted from Belden's salvage in this shipwreck. It provided him with goods for his own store in Monterey.

78 The grant was to the Rancho Barranca Colorado. As pointed out in *note* 60, *ante*, the acreage totaled 21,000 acres.

79 Belden, writing to John Cooper from San José, November 29, 1845, informed him that he was leaving for Sacramento. *Larkin Papers*, IV, 109. On December 10, Belden arrived at Sutter's Fort, the same day John C. Frémont arrived on his second California excursion. December 16, Belden departed for the upper valley in company with McVicker and several other companions. *New Helvetia Diary*, pp. 16, 18.

80 On March 1, 1846, Belden arrived at Sutter's "in a canoe from the upper part of the [Sacramento] valley . . .," and on the 3rd departed in the same conveyance. *Ibid.*, p. 29.

81 In March, 1846, Captain John Paty leased his ship the *Don Quixote*, to Governor Don José Castro for the purpose of bringing supplies to California from Mexico. Since Paty had just arrived from the Hawaiian Islands with a full cargo, he unloaded his ship, leaving part of the merchandise in Yerba Buena, the rest in Monterey. He appointed Belden agent in the former, and his nephew, James Gleason, in the latter pueblo. Belden left Monterey around the first of April to take up his post in Yerba Buena. He was also empowered by Captain Paty to collect debts due him in the Bay area. Gleason to his sister; to William Paty, March 30, April [1?], 1846. *Gleason Letters*, pp. 21-23.

Apparently Belden continued to collect debts owed to his abortive store enterprise of 1845. Josiah Belden Store Receipts, February 11-October 8, 1846; José María Amado to Belden, September 21, 1846. *Vallejo Papers*, HEH.

82 Captain Paty's ship was the *Don Quixote*. *Davis Recollections*, pp. 191-193, provides an unusual sketch.

83 Goods shipped to California via Mexican ports were taxed. Since the Sandwich Islands were an independent kingdom, the creation of duty free ports greatly increased profits and enhanced effective

competition for traders engaged in Hawaiian-California commerce. Captain John Paty held a virtual monopoly on that commerce until 1846. In that year he was challenged by Captain Thomas Russom's brig, *Euphemia*. In 1847, the *Mary Ann* began to ply the same trade route. By 1848 three additional ships entered the lists, the *S.S.*, the *Starling*, and *Louisa*. Because of the advent of serious rivals, Paty retired, leaving his nephew James Gleason to close out his affairs. *Ibid., pp.* 407-408; Gleason to Belden, August 2; to Captain John Paty, August 22, 1846; to his sister May 2, 1847. *Gleason Letters,* pp. 32-34, 36-40.

"Journal of Captain John Paty, 1807-1868," edited by Mrs. Edward C. Green, *CHSQ,* XIV (1935), 291-346, vividly describes his activities. Hereafter cited *Paty Journal.*

84 It is difficult to ascertain the identity of this ship. The best surmise would be Captain Francisco Unamano's brig, the *Constante. Davis Recollections,* 407; Bancroft, IV, 564, *note.*

85 Belden's date is in error. By 1848, Paty had closed out his affairs along the coast, but continued to do partial business from Oahu with California. Paty to Larkin, January 8, September 12; Larkin to Paty, September 6, 1847. *Larkin Papers,* VI, 316, 336; James Gleason to Paty, August 22, 1848. *Gleason Letters,* p. 43; *Paty Journal,* pp. 329-338.

86 Davis's ship, the *Euphemia,* made its first trip under his ownership in March, 1846, and returned in the fall of 1847; again in 1848. Later it was sold to the city of San Francisco for use as a floating prison.

Davis states that Belden assisted him as early as the spring of 1846 in disposing of land around the Bay area. Their mutual acquaintance dated back to 1842 when Belden was Larkin's agent at Santa Cruz. *Davis Recollections,* pp. 265, 408; Frank Soulé, *et al., The Annals of San Francisco,* p. 223; John Paty to Larkin, July 16, 1852. *Larkin Papers,* I, 249.

87 Davis relates that he met Belden at San Pedro in early 1847, probably in February. The two took passage along with another companion for Monterey on board the *Euphemia.* Because of stiff headwinds, Davis, Belden, and a third companion, Louis McLane left the ship at Point Concepcíon where they headed inland. After borrowing horses from the Cojo Ranch of Don

Anastasio Carrillo, they proceeded to William G. Dana's Rancho Nipomo. From him they were able to purchase horses, returning their borrowed animals to Carrillo, and continued overland to Monterey in the company of Dr. Nicholas A. Den and H. F. Teschemacher. *Ibid.*, p. 292; *Davis Papers,* Box 8, and *Abel Stearns Papers,* Box 83, HEH.

Belden had undoubtedly accompanied Davis on his business trip south to collect from John C. Frémont money due for supplies that had been purchased. Andrew Rolle, *An American in California*: *The Biography of William Heath Davis* . . ., pp. 52-55, explains business affairs with Frémont, but differs on the circumstances of Davis's return trip to the north.

Belden was back in San José by March. By late spring he was in Yerba Buena handling real estate matters for Larkin. Belden to Larkin, March 31, September 2; Larkin to Belden, August 10, 14, 1847. *Larkin Papers,* VI, 79, 263, 271-272, 306; *Davis Papers,* Box 8, HEH. Belden to Davis, November 18, 1846; May 15, November 6, 1847. *Davis Papers,* CSL.

88 Belden opened his store in the spring of 1848, Mellus & Howard being his silent partners. He maintained that relationship for two years when he sold out. Phelps, I, 249; Shuck, p. 927.

89 This probably was Isaac Branham who came to San José in 1846. Hall, pp. 368-369. *Belden Papers* in the possession of Clyde Arbuckle point the year 1849 as the date Belden sold his mercantile business.

90 Belden married Sarah Margaret Jones, February 1, 1849. She was the daughter of Zachariah Jones who came to California in the 1846 emigration.

91 Belden became Mayor, April 13, 1850, serving a one year term. In 1851 he served another one year term as Councilman. *San José City Archives,* 15.

Belden, along with 19 other prominent citizens of San José, signed a note for $34,000 in order to provide quarters for the 1849 legislature. The site was on property owned by Belden. Hall, p. 206.

Chester S. Lyman, *Around the Horn to the Sandwich Islands* . . ., p. 288, an eyewitness to the marriage, wrote in his journal: "Thurs. [Feb. 1st] Returned to Pueblo [San José]. Eve[ning].

Mr. Belden married Miss Margaret Jones by Mr. [Kimball H.]
Dimmick, Alcalde; awkward affair, hands not joined, very stiff.
After the ceremony full supper, table cleared 7 times. Married in
the bar room. Large crowd. At 9 adjourned to Mr. Cook's & had a
fandango . . . Oceans of wine & brandy, & most of the company
drunk, too. Broke up at 5 [in the] morning." (Punctuation
partially supplied.)

Belden's wife was later described as "a very conscientious
woman, beloved by all who knew her." Dickenson, p. 108.

92 John Cooper married Encarnación and Leese married Rosalía.

93 Captain John B. Frisbie, who came to California with the New
York Volunteers during the Mexican War, married Epefanía. Two
years later his brother, Dr. Levi Frisbie, married Adelayda.
Myrtle M. McKittrick, *Vallejo, Son of California,* p. 307.

94 Sketches of each of the above mentioned can be found in Bancroft's "Pioneer Register."

95 Bancroft amply covers the military battles of the Mexican War
in California. The best eye-witness account of the battle of San
Pasqual is found in the diary of Dr. John S. Griffin, edited by
George W. Ames, Jr., *CHSQ,* XXI (1942), 333-342.

96 Belden's account here lends little dimension to that already
established.

97 Elliott Libbey, captain of the *Tasso,* 1845-1848, also the *Commodore Shubrick* in 1847, was not killed in the incident alluded
to by Belden. Arriving in Yerba Buena in October, 1845, some
of the *Tasso's* crew went ashore and were attacked by a band of
ruffians made up of members of the Sanchez family. Informed
of this, Libbey in company with Nathan Spear, the supercargo,
put ashore to investigate the affair late on the night of October
11th. Soon after, they were attacked by some "seven or eight
ruffians. Mr. Spear was knocked down by a number of blows,
and Capt. Libbey was stabbed in the breast and back, his head
cut open by a sabre, his face mutilated." Left lying in the street
for dead, he was taken to Spear's home for treatment. This
incident was used, as Paul Peterson wrote to W. D. M. Howard:
"To stimulate the authorities to energetick measures, I have
made Capt. Lebbies [Libbey] case appe[a]r mortal, but in reality
I believe him out of danger, still he was most dreadfully cut and

beaten and but for a man named Osia would been murdered."
Efforts on the part of Thomas O. Larkin to bring the accused to
justice failed. One side effect, however, may have been Larkin's
swift action in appointing William A. Leidesdorff to the post of
vice-counsel for San Francisco. *Larkin Papers,* IV, 16, *et seq.;*
letters to W. D. M. Howard from Larkin, October 18; Captain
T. C. Everett, October 19; Peterson's, October 21, 1845. *W. D. M.
Howard Papers,* CHS.

98 Need it be remarked, this is on old wives' tale. Rain was plentiful
in 1840, 1842, 1845 seasons, but 1841 and 1843 were very severe
drought years.

99 John C. Jones, writing to Larkin from Santa Barbara, November
7, 1841, commented on Mexican food: "There is plenty of Corn
to be obtained, on which I could feast, would it make its appearance in the shape of good old Yankee pudding or even a hoe
cake baked before a negroes shins, but when it comes before me
in the form of such horrible cakes as constitutes the bread of this
country, ye Gods, at the very sight of them, my throat becomes
as dry as the clnk of a lime kiln, and to attempt to pass one of
them into my inner man would be as impossible, as to find a fit
man in California for Governor of the Department." *Larkin
Papers,* I, 134.

100 Grove Cook, a "likable but wild young man" from Callaway
County, Missouri, married Sophronia Fullen Sublette, sister to
the famed *mountain men,* the Sublette brothers, March 31, 1825.
In subsequent years, he occupied himself with raising mules which
he readily sold to his enterprising brother-in-law, William. On
March 29, 1841, Sophronia brought divorce proceedings against
her husband, charging that he had "been guilty of gross and
wanton ill treatment towards [her] . . . and [had] offered such
indignities to said complainant, as to render her condition intoler-
able." Further, she charged, "that said Grove [had] for more
than two years past been guilty of and addicted to habitual
drunkenness: That he [had] abandoned [her] . . . and refused to
support her." The decree was granted without contest, October 4,
1841, and Sophronia was given custody of their only child Theresa.
On April 20, 1843, Sophronia died and Theresa Cook perished in
the 1849 St. Louis cholera epidemic.

In the midst of his wife's divorce suit, Grove Cook, apparently destitute, was able to join the Bartleson party. *Dawson Narrative*, pp. 9-11, 43, commented that Cook "begged to be allowed to pay his way by driving [a] wagon," thus enabling him to work his way west to California. On arrival at Dr. Marsh's, Cook joined Belden in traveling to San José. And it was there he took root.

Acquiring a distillery, he began to amass a personal fortune; he acquired the Rancho de los Capitancillos and exploited a quicksilver mine discovered on his property. In 1845 when Solomon Sublette guided a party to California, he informed Cook of Sophronia's final divorce decree and subsequent death. Immediately after, Cook married Miss Rebecca Kelsey at Sutter's Fort, December 8, 1845.

Later, when Andrew Sublette came to San José, ill and destitute, Cook cared for his former brother-in-law. Together they invested in a southern California gold mine that proved financial ruin to both. Cook died in poverty, February, 1852.

These biographical facts are drawn from: John E. Sunder, *Bill Sublette*, p. 73, *et seq.*; Hall, pp. 136-137; Doyce B. Nunis, Jr., "The Enigma of the Sublette Overland Party, 1845," *Pacific Historical Review*, XXVIII (1959), 341-341, *notes;* ———, *Andrew Sublette, Rocky Mountain Prince*, Chs. VI-VII; Clyde Arbuckle, "Grove C. Cook of San José," *Westways*, 43 (December, 1951), p. 19; *Alta California*, February 1, 1852.

101 Hiram Teal came to California in 1841, a member of the Oregon Company that arrived that year. He procured a stock of goods from Larkin via Mazatlan, and kept a store in Yerba Buena from 1841-1843. Because his business was a failure, his loss running to over a thousand dollars, he left California in 1843, for Mexico via Hawaii. Teal to Larkin, September 7, 1841, and April 3 [?], 1842. *Larkin Papers*, I, 117, 186.

102 Paul Bailey, *Sam Brannan and the California Mormons*, treats that subject extensively. The *Brooklyn* left New York, February 4, 1846, with 238 "Saints" on board, and arrived in San Francisco on July 31, after an eventful passage.

William A. Bartell reported the Mormons' arrival to Edward M. Kern, August 6, 1846. He appraised Brannan as a man of "limited education (a practical pirate) .

Three Belden Letters

From the *Coe Collection,* Yale University Library
[Josiah Belden to Mrs. Eliza M. Bowers.]

MONTEREY, CALIFORNIA
DEC. 21, 1841.

Dear Sister:

I HAVE AT LAST the pleasure to inform of my arrival in California. We reached here on the 4th of November after being 6 months lacking a week on the way. We were much longer coming from the Rocky Mountains where I wrote you last, than we expected to be owing to our not knowing the way and in fact there were times when we scarcely expected to get here at all or anywhere else and almost made up our minds to starve to death in the mountains. We kept wa[n]dering on over mountains valleys and rivers. Sometimes in one direction and sometimes in another without knowing whether we were right or wrong until we got nearly out of provisions and found winter approaching when we concluded to leave our wagons and take the cattle that drawed some of them to eat. We then packed our things on our horses and pushed along as fast as we could until we at last struck St. Mary's River which we had been directed to follow down to where it emptied into a lake and then we struck into the California mountains. In coming down Mary's River we frequently fell in [with] large parties of Indians and were several times in expectation of being attacked by them but I suppose they saw that we were well prepared for them and thought it best to let us alone. When we got to the mouth of Mary's River we hired two Indians for guides to take us across the mountains but the scoundrels led us into the very worst part of the mountains and then ran away in the night and left us there. We were then in a most discouraging situation. We were in an unknown wilderness enclosed by mountains on every side rising to an immense height and covered with snow. To that there seemed to be no possibility of getting over them and when myself and another climbed to the top of one of them we could see nothing but mountains upon mountains as far as the eye could reach in the direction we wanted to go. We could not turn back as we knew we should starve before we could get back to where there was anything to eat for we were then just eating our last ox and there was no game to be found in the country.

We, however, toiled along slowly up and down the mountains for 22 days when we at last came out onto the plains almost worn down with hunger and fatigue. We had to walk nearly all the way over the mountains and throw away many of our things as our poor horses could hardly scramble up the steep rocky precipices without anything on them. Some of them slipped on the sides of the steep mountains and were pitched down headlong and dashed to pieces among the rocks. We had to kill some of our horses and eat them as we had nothing else to eat except acorns for about 2 weeks. We however worked our way through it and in 5 days after we got out on to the plains of California we came to the house of an American farmer. We rested there two days and then a part of us started for one of the towns 45 miles off. But what was our surprise on arriving there to find ourselves all made prisoners by the

government. The law here requires that every foreigner
coming into the country shall bring a passport from the
country he leaves and as we had no passports to show we
were arrested and our arms taken away from us. They put
us in the guard house but did not keep us too [long].
[W]e had liberty to go out and in when we chose but were
not allowed to leave the town. They kept us so 6 days
when they set us at liberty and gave us passports to travel
about the country by our getting some Americans who are
living here to go security for our good behavior whilst we
are in the country. Myself and one more then left there
and came to this place. This is a fine country and a most
delightful healthy climate. It is hardly ever cold enough
here in the winter to make a fire necessary for comfort. I
like the country better than the Spanish people who live
here for many of them are great rogues as I can testify for
they stole 4 horses from myself and my friend at the town
where we were arrested. Some of the Spaniards though
have treated us very hospitably and the Americans we have
found here have treated us very well. Our company have
now scattered themselves about the country seeking employment and most of them I believe have gone to work,
some in one place and some in another.

I am at present working a little here at my trade but
there is not much to do at that and I shall soon have to look
out for something to do. I have some prospect of getting
employment as clerk in a store but it is uncertain. If I do,
I shall probably stay here a year. If not I expect I shall
go home in the spring. This place is situated on the Pacific
Ocean and there are at present several American vessels
here. P.S. I have just made an engagement with Mr. Larkin to go clerk in a store for a year. I do not get much
wages this year but if I choose to stay another, I have a

chance of doing better. I don't think I shall stay another year unless I see a chance of making a fortune. I hope you will write to me immediately. Send your letter by a private hand if you can hear of any chance. If not, put it in the mail but if you put it in the mail you must pay 25¢ postage. When you put it in the office or else it will not come, direct your letter to the care of Mr. Thomas O. Larkin, Monterey, California . . .

[Envelope addressed to Mrs. Eliza M. Bowers, Upper Middletown, Conn., United States of America. (Postmarked: NEW YORK - Mar. 25).]

[Written along the margin of page one:]

Direct your letter like this—Mr. Josiah Belden, Upper California care of Mr. Henry A. Pierce, Charlestown, Massachusetts and pay postage and he will send it. I have written to Susan and sent the letter by sea so that if this is lost she may get the other.

II

SANTA CRUZ, CALIFORNIA
MARCH 21ST, 1842

Dear Sister:

A S SOME OF THE MEN who came here with me are about to return to the States, I gladly embrace the opportunity of writing you a few lines. I wrote to you and Susan about two months since but I am doubtful whether the letter will ever reach you. I sent yours across the land by the way of Mexico and Susan's by sea so as to have a chance both ways. In my other letters I told you something of my journey here but in case you do not receive them I will just say that we were six months on the road and had a pretty hard time of it. In the latter part of the journey we had a very good prospect of starving to death and the only way we lived was by killing our horses and mules and eating them and going afoot. We got through it however at last and glad enough we were to get once more where people lived and where there was something to eat. I first went to Monterey the capitol of the country where I stayed about two months and as there was at that time no chance for me to get back to the States and as I was about out of money I thought best to accept of an offer made me by Mr. Larkin, an American merchant there, to come to this place and take charge of a store. I had to engage for a year or nothing and at a small salary, but I thought that was better than to come to want in a strange country. He says he will give me a share in the business next year if I choose to stay, but I think I shall go home when this year is up. At all events, I shall not stay here unless I see a chance of doing well by it for I had rather live at home among my friends than in a foreign country and amongst people that don't speak my own language.

I have unfortunately always had a great inclination for rambling about but I think I am pretty well cured of it now. I suppose you and Susan too have blamed me much for coming here and I have often blamed myself, but it can't be helped now and I must just make the best I can of it. I am in hopes that by the time I get back to the States it will be better times there so that I can make a living in one place and be content to stay there. This place is on the north side of Monterey Bay, close by the Pacific ocean and about 20 miles across from Monterey which is on the other side of the bay. It can hardly be called a town or even a village, there is so little of it. It has formerly been a Roman catholic missionary established for civilizing the wild Indians, and has once been very flourishing, but it is now broken up and fast going to decay though there is still

some trade here amongst the few Indians that remain and
the farmers and other that are about here. There is only
one foreigner in the place besides myself though there are
a few others living around within a few miles of here. I was
a great deal puzzled when I first came by having to do business with people who spoke a language that I knew nothing about, but I have now got so that I can jabber spanish
pretty smartly and make out better. I don't know but they
will make a catholic of me before I go away as I have my
store along side of the church and am boarding with the
catholic priest, though I think the old fellow knows my
opinions most too well to try to convert me. He is a clever
jolly fellow who is as fond of his glass, his cards and his
jokes as any man. The people here are generally pretty
clever to a man's face, though most of them would not
hesitate to rob him the minute his back is turned. I have
managed to get along pretty well with them so far and
shall try to continue to do so. Notwithstanding they are
great rogues, they are generally pretty hospitable, free
hearted and sociable and I enjoy myself pretty well
amongst them and to their hospitality. I suppose you will
think they have rather an awkward way of showing it when
I tell you that every person who is traveling has to carry
his blanket with him and when he stops at a farmer's house
at night, as he has to do (for there are no taverns in the
country) he must just spread his blanket on the floor, roll
himself up in it and take the best nap he can. When the
supper is ready the family sit by the fire on some wooden
blocks or something else and each one receives his plate of
vi[c]tuals, which among the poor people they generally
eat with their fingers. However, such is the custom of the
country and it seems to be done with a good will. I have
pretty fine times here as I have not much to do and a horse

to ride about whenever I wish and as beautiful a country to ride over too as the sun ever shone on. Besides I have plenty of lively bright-eyed Spanish girls to chat with so that one way with another I enjoy myself tolerable well.

If Susan is there this will do for both of you, for I shall not have time to write as the man that takes it is off very soon. Give my best to Susan when you write to her if she is not there and tell her to write to me. Give my respects to Mr. Bowers and all our friends there. Do not fail of writing to me soon. When you write direct your letter to me in care of Thomas O. Larkin, Monterey, California. Then wrap it in another sheet of paper seal it and direct on the outside to Mr. Henry Pierce, Charlestown, Massachusetts and pay the postage on it to that place. He will take off the outside cover and send it on.

Adios,
Yours affectionate brother
J. BELDEN

III

MONTEREY, CALIFORNIA
JUNE 15, 1845

Dear Sister:

I RECEIVED a few days since, from Mr. Larkin, Uncle Russel's letter to him dated February 1844; and you may judge that it gave me the greatest pleasure, as I had not heard a word from you since I left the United States, and did not know whether you were dead or alive. To know that I still have two sisters, and other relatives alive and well and to hear from them while I am away in a foreign country is, I assure you, a great satisfaction to me. Besides the letter of March 1842, which Uncle Russel mentions having received from me, I have written several others but

as I have never until now received any answer I had almost
given up hope of ever hearing from you, and began to fear
you were all dead. I believe I wrote in my letter of 1842
which you received, that when I had completed the year for
which I was engaged with Mr. Larkin, I should probably
return home, but at the expiration of that time I found
myself unable to do so and continued nearly another year
in the same employ, I then opened a small store for myself
in which I have been engaged up to the present time, but
I am now about to give it up as it has not proved very
profitable to me; have trusted out the most of my small
stock, and now, on account of the revolution which has
lately taken place here and other circumstances, I am unable to collect my debts, so I shall probably lose nearly all
I have made. I hardly know at present what I shall go at
next. I think of making a small attempt at for a few days
as I know of two or three places where silver has been
found and I have some hopes of being able to make it
profitable, but it is very uncertain. If I fail in that perhaps
I may try to make a new start in a store, as there is now
some prospect of our soon having better times. We have
just received news that there will soon be a force of 2,000
soldiers and a new Governor here from Mexico, which will
make more business and make money more plenty, which
has been very scarce lately. About six months since the
people of the country raised a revolution against the Mexican Governor and his officers and drove him out of the
country with about 200 Mexican soldiers that he had here.
It appears that the Mexican Government are now determined to put down the people who raised the revolution
and for that purpose are now sending the above mentioned
force here. The Californians say they will rise in the body
and prevent the Mexicans from coming into the country,

but I think the Mexicans will be too strong for them. At all events, I suppose we will have another small touch of civil war; but if they do not fight better than they did in the late revolution there will not be much damage done, except what property they steal and destroy, for they fought two days without killing or wounding a single man. I believe four or five horses were killed during the fight which was all the blood that was shed. For about three weeks during the war I had the honor to command a company of four Americans who were stationed in the Governor's house every night to defend his wife and his house against any sudden attack of the Californians, as he had more confidence in us than in her own country people. There were from 70 to 100 of the Californians encamped in the neighborhood of the town, and one day they said they were coming in to attack the place, so we got all ready for a fight but their courage failed them, so they did not attempt it. I received about fifty dollars for my services, and the other four men in proportion, and I suppose we were about the only ones that made anything by the revolution —though I can't say I made anything by it on the whole, for they stole five or six horses from me in the meantime. In the future if they have any more fighting to do they may do it themselves for all me, unless I fight like Davy Crockets on my own hook to keep them from robbing me.

I often think about going home, but I don't know when I shall be able to do it. I almost begin to think the California proverb true, which says that after a foreigner has been here one year he can never get away. However, I am determined if God spares my life and gives me health to see my native town again before a great while. The fact is I have now been away so long I feel ashamed to go home poor; and in the hope of bettering my condition by some means I still hold on here. I often think of you and particularly of Susan, who, I fear may stand in need of some assistance, which I know it is my duty, as much as it would be my pleasure to render her if it was in my power; but although I have never been a spendthrift, and have always done my best to get ahead in the world, yet I have not been able to so far do more than just make a living and keep even. But I still hope that be exertions and some better turn of fortune I shall be able before long to make you both happy, and rest assured that if such should be the case you will find that I am still a brother to you; and that, although at present, a long distance off I do not forget you. Probably I shall remain here some months or a year longer to see if there is any better prospect and if not I m[igh]t then either go home or go to South America. Whatever I do I shall always write to you and let you know where I am. I have become a citizen of this country by naturalization which I did to enable me to hold real estate, which I could not do without it; but that will make no difference about my remaining in the country. I have obtained from the Government a grant of a tract of land containing twenty one thousand acres, said to be some of the best land in the country, though I have never seen it myself as it is on the river Sacramento nearly 300 miles from Monterey. I expected to have been able to put 200 head of young cows on it this fall, for the purpose of raising stock but I can't do it from the impossibility of collecting my debts. The land was given to me by the Government but cost me about $100 expense in the form of law, maps, etc. I am in hopes it will be worth a lot to me some day though at present it is not considered very valuable on account of the country not being much settled there.

Give my best respects to Uncle Russel and tell him I can

not sufficiently thank him for the interest he has shown in my welfare by writing to Mr. Larkins concerning me. Also remember me to Aunt McKee, Henry, Joseph and all the family. Ask Abigail's boys Francis and Frederick if they remember me yet. Give my respects to Emily and her family and all other friends. Remember me to Mr. Bowers and tell him I shall be there some of these days to see how many little Bowers he has got.

Eliza, I fancy you must be getting to be an old woman by this time for I am getting grey headed and you are five years older than I am. Susan, I suppose you too have got to be quite an old maid now. Oh! how I want to see you all to see what changes time has made. I address this to Eliza because I am not certain where Susan is, but consider it as written to both of you. Get Uncle Russel to direct the letters as he did to the care of Mr. Thomas [O.] Larkin, American Consul. Tell Uncle Russel I should like to have him write to me often and tell me how things go on in that part of the country.

Yours ever affectionate brother,
JOSIAH BELDEN.

The 1841 Caravan: A Census Summary

Company Rosters

The Missionary Party and Associates

Thomas Fitzpatrick

Jesuit Fathers: Pierre-Jean De Smet, Nicholas
Point, Gregory Mengarini

Trappers: Jim Baker, John Gray, William Mast,
Piga (a Frenchman)

Pleasure seekers: Amos E. Frye, Rogers, Romaine
(an Englishman)

Teamsters: five in number. Here must be included
the three Jesuit lay brothers: William
Claessens, Charles Huet, Joseph Specht.

Lone traveler: Reverend Joseph Williams

The Bartleson Party

Those who arrived in California:

John Bartleson

Elias Barnett

Josiah Belden

William Belty

John Bidwell

Henry L. Brolaski

David W. Chandler

Joseph B. Chiles

Grove C. Cook
James Dawson
Nicholas Dawson
Paul Geddes, alias Talbot H. Green
George Henshaw
Charles Hopper
Henry Huber
James John
Thomas Jones
Andrew Kelsey
Benjamin Kelsey
Mrs. Nancy A. Kelsey, and her young daughter
John McDowell
Green McMahon
Nelson McMahon
Michael C. Nye
A. Gwinn Patton
Robert Rickman
John Roland
John L. Schwartz
James P. Springer
Robert H. Thomes
Ambrose Walton
Major Walton
Charles M. Weber

Those who went to Oregon:
—— Carrol
John De Smart
Richard Fillan [Phelan] and wife (Mrs. Gray)
    and her child by former marriage
Charles W. Flügge
David F. Hill

Isaac Kelsey and wife (daughter of Richard
    Williams)
Samuel Kelsey, wife and five children
William P. Overton
Edward Rogers
James Ross
William Towler
Richard Williams and wife
Those who left the company prior to the division at
Soda Springs:
——— Jones
Henry Peyton
George Simpson
George Shotwell, deceased
Elisha Stone

Commentary

The number of members of this caravan has been subject
to disputation. Bidwell, *Journey,* pp. 1-2, declares there
were 64 men in addition to women and children. In later
recollections, he gives various figures (ranging from 64
as the total complement to declaring that the missionary
party had some 17-18 men, in addition to his own group).
Bidwell, *Echoes,* pp. 22, 37-38.

Dawson Narrative, p. 9, presents the figure at 100. Fr.
De Smet (*Letters,* I, 280), under date of May 19, 1841,
fixes the number at 70, carefully noting that 50 of the
company could manage a rifle. (It should be noted that
Fr. De Smet's estimate would exclude the seven men who
joined the company several days later. This would raise
his figure to 76.) Charles Hopper claims there were 76
C. A. Menefee, *Historical and Descriptive Sketches . . .,*
p.149. Reverend Joseph Williams (*Williams Narrative,*

p. 219), the last person to join the west bound party (May 26th), presents the figure of 50. Bancroft, IV, 268, states that at the beginning there were 48 men and 15 women and children in the Bartleson party, while there were 14 members in the Jesuit band, a total of 77 in all.

Caughey, p. 209; Robert G. Cleland, *From Wilderness to Empire*, p. 179, agree on the number 69 for the Bartleson party.

The missionary party's complement seems to be rather accurately established. Bidwell, *Journey*, pp. 1-2, specifically notes that the group consisted of eleven members, and he includes in that number: Fitzpatrick, the three Jesuit priests, John Gray, Romaine, and the five teamsters. He then lists, separately, the three trappers, Baker, Piga, and William Mast; the pleasure seekers, A. E. Frye and Rogers, along with the Rev. Williams bound on a visit to Oregon. In a later recollection, written in 1889, he listed the party as composed of Fitzpatrick, the three Jesuit priests, "and ten or eleven French Canadians," in addition to John Gray, Baker, and "a young Englishman named Romaine." Bidwell, *California*, pp. 15-16, a census which must be dismissed because of an apparent lapse of memory on this score.

Thus, from Bidwell's 1841 accounting, based on his journal, the missionary party, taking his roster as an accurate measure of that party's number, we find there were 17 grouped in its membership. *De Smet Letters*, I, 276, 278, sheds little light on this census problem. Father Mengarini, writing years later, mentions only John Gray, Romaine, and states there were six Canadian mule-drivers. (Partoll, p. 4.) Here, because of the time lapse, we must discount the number of drivers.

The first doubt cast on Bidwell's reported census is

that Piga might well have been one of the teamsters, rather than an independent trapper. We must also assume that the number of teamsters included the three Jesuit lay brothers. *De Smet Letters,* I, 300-301.

Another question is posed by the mere mention of Rogers, for in the roster of the Bartleson party members an Edward Rogers is listed as belonging to that group. Yet, Bidwell lists the name of Rogers also among the missionary party. It can be assumed only that there were two men of that name in the beginning caravan.

Of the missionary party, six left the company before the caravan reached Soda Springs. William Mast took his leave while the company was at Fort Laramie, June 22. When Henry Fraeb's trapper party was encountered on the Green River, July 25, Jim Baker cast his lot with them, while Frye, Gray, Rogers, and Romaine decided to return to St. Louis, or the United States, as Bidwell relates in his *Journey,* pp. 8, 11. In his later memoirs, Bidwell, *California,* p. 25, merely lists Rogers (spelling it Rodgers) and Amos E. Frye as turning back, although he notes that Peyton, one of his own party, joined them. In his *Journal,* p. 11, Bidwell enters under date of July 25 the fact that seven of the caravan left that body, listing Gray, Frye, Rogers (?), Romaine, and Baker, names found in his previous missionary roster, and adding the name of Jones, who was apparently a member of his own caravan, along with Peyton as turning back to St. Louis. *Williams Narrative,* p. 231, records merely that six members left the company on the Green in late July. Fr. De Smet (*Letters,* I, 295) says five or six turned back along with Romaine. *Dawson Narrative,* p. 14, lists Frye, Gray, Romaine, and "a few others" as turning back.

It would appear from Bidwell's *Journey* that the missionary party was diminished prior to the Soda Springs split between the two companies by the loss of Baker, Frye, Gray, Mast, Rogers, and Romaine, thus reducing their original number from 17 to 11.

Of the Bartleson party, it is safe to observe that those members who are listed in the California-bound roster were in the company from the beginning and did arrive in California at Marsh's ranch, November 4, 1841. Bidwell in his *Journey,* p. 14, under date of August 11, notes that 32 men, one woman and child, a total of 34, headed for California. This is confirmed by Nicholas Dawson and in the roster of emigrants given to the California authorities by Marsh, wherein he notes the arrival of 31 men, one woman and child, coupled with the independent arrival of the missing member, James John, who made Sutter's Fort. *Dawson MS,* Bancroft Library; Bidwell, *Echoes,* p. 75.

That group of the Bartleson party which elected to go to Oregon, when the missionary party headed north to Fort Hall from Soda Springs, is more difficult to appraise with certainty. Accepting Bidwell's roster as presented in his *Journey,* p. 1, and substantiated, to some extent in his 1889 recollections (Bidwell, *California,* p. 26, *note*), the listing presented above seems to be accurate, with these exceptions.

There is an area of possible doubt over the entry of two names, Jones and Rogers. Bidwell, *Journey,* p. 1, lists three separate entries for the name Jones: Thomas, J. M., and simply, Jones. Of the Joneses, we are sure that Thomas Jones reached California (Bancroft, IV, 695). As to J. M. Jones and plain Mr. Jones, doubts arise. On July 25, Bidwell records (*Journey,* p. 11) that a "Jones" elected to return to St. Louis with Frye, Gray, Peyton, Rogers, and Romaine. No other entries elucidate which

Jones this was. It can only be assumed that one of the two latter Joneses elected to return to the United States while one continued on to Oregon, this being J. M. Jones. *John Diary* lists a Jones as returning.

The same plight plagues the entry of the name Rogers. Bidwell, *Journey,* pp. 1-2, lists an Edward Rogers in the Bartleson party and a "Rogers" in the missionary company who was on a "pleasure excursion." Under entry of July 25, on the Green River, Bidwell (*ibid.*, p. 11) enters the name of "Rogers" as returning with Frye, Gray, Jones, Peyton, and Romaine to St. Louis. *John Diary* concurs with this list. From this, it would appear that Edward Rogers cast his fortunes with the Oregon bound party, while the pleasure seeking "Rogers" returned east. In his 1889 account, Bidwell (*California,* p. 25) lists a "Rogers" as returning east.

In Bidwell's original roster (*Journey,* p. 1), there is no listing for a Mrs. Gray, a widow with child. On July 30, Mrs. Gray, a sister to one of the Mrs. Kelseys (and internal evidence leads this writer to believe it was Mrs. Samuel Kelsey), was married by Father De Smet to Richard Fillan [Phelan] (whom Bidwell calls Cocrum, describing him as a man with one eye) who had joined the party at Fort Laramie. *Ibid.,* p. 4. Apparently they ventured on to Oregon, since it would appear that Fillan's [Phelan] wife was the sister of Mrs. Samuel Kelsey whose husband did emigrate with his wife and family to Oregon. This new family, the Fillans [Phelans], then, must be added to the Oregon party. The best treatment of the Kelseys to date is given in two articles written by Mrs. Eugene F. Fountain, published in the Blue Lake [Calif.] *Advocate,* June 13, 20, 1957. Copies sent to this writer by Mrs. Fountain of Arcata, California.

In a later recollection (1889), Bidwell, *California,* p. 26, *note,* records that Richard Williams and wife; Samuel Kelsey, wife and five children; Isaac (Josiah or Isaiah) Kelsey and wife (daughter of Richard Williams, who was married on the trail either May 31 or June 1 by the Reverend Joseph Williams, *Williams Narrative,* pp. 221-222; Bidwell, *Journey,* p. 4); C. W. Flügge; Fowler; Williams (the Methodist Episcopal minister); "Cheyenne" Dawson, "'Bear" Dawson headed for Oregon. The last two listings are in conflict with the roster of California emigrant arrivals and must be discounted. The two Dawsons were not related. Both came to California with Bidwell. *Dawson Narrative,* pp. 12, 43. The list presented above would seem to be accurate for the Bartleson Oregon bound emigrants. This would place the number in that roster at 23.

However, in tabulating the census for the 1841 caravan, three other problems need to be clarified, in particular the Bartleson company. Since Bancroft indicates (IV, 268) that there were 15 women and children, this figure must be examined.

There were five women in the company, this is clear: Mrs. Benjamin (Nancy A.) Kelsey, Mrs. Samuel Kelsey, Mrs. Richard Williams, Mrs. Gray (who married Fillan [Phelan]), and Miss Williams (who married Isaac Kelsey).

The statements of the number of children in the emigrant train, from the consulted records, totals only seven. These were: the child of Mrs. Gray, the child of Mrs. Benjamin Kelsey, the five children of Mrs. Samuel Kelsey. The family of Richard Williams, other than the daughter who married Fillan [Phelan], as to number, is no where indicated. It could be assumed that since the

Williams' had a daughter of marrying age, there were younger children in their family. Excluding Miss Williams from the category of children, this would definitely fix the number at seven. Adding the five women in the party, the total figure would be 12. If Bancroft's figure of 15 women and children is correct, this would imply that the Williams' family had three other offspring.

A third problem is the entry made by Bidwell at Fort Laramie. There he entered, June 22, the fact that two men had joined them, along with an Indian family, to travel to the Green River. *Journey,* p. 8. Assuredly one of these men was Richard Fillan [Phelan] (whom Bidwell calls Cocrum and James John, Cockrel) who married Mrs. Gray on July 23, and in all probability went on to settle in Oregon. As for the second man, there is no name nor subsequent reference, so we can only assume he left the company at the Green and never entered into Bidwell's Oregon bound roster.

As to the members of the Bartleson party who decided to return east prior to Soda Springs where the company split, the number can be fixed at four. Elisha Stone was the first to give up the trip, returning on June 5 with a band of American Fur Company trappers. George Simpson elected to withdraw at Fort Laramie, June 22. Jones and Henry Peyton made their decision on July 25 on the Green River, joining the departing missionary party members, Baker, Frye, Gray, Rogers, and Romaine. Bidwell, *Journey,* pp. 5, 8, 11. The *Daily Missouri Republican,* September 28, 1841, noted that nine or ten returned.

Lastly, one of the Bartleson party became a casualty, George Shotwell, who accidentally shot himself June 13 and was buried. Bidwell, *Journey* p. 7.

Accepting the lists and exceptions as presented above,

these conclusions can be reached:

First. The original Bartleson company definitely consisted of 60 persons, with the possibility of at least three additional children in the Williams' family.

Second. The California bound contingent is accurately fixed at the number 34, while the Oregon bound emigrees totaled at least 22, with the possibility of three additional children in the Williams' family.

Third. Four of the Bartleson party definitely returned east, and a fifth died, his place being taken by Fillan who joined up at Fort Laramie to become a member of the Oregon bound faction.

Fourth. The missionary party had a beginning complement of 17 members, losing six before they reached Soda Springs.

Accepting these conclusions, it would appear that the original 1841 west bound caravan had a complement of 77 souls. By the time the caravan reached Soda Springs, that number was reduced to 67, if we include the possibility of three additional Williams' children, or 64 without that consideration.

At the dividing place of the joint caravan, Soda Springs, Bidwell, *Journey,* p. 14, simply recorded, August 11, that 32 men, one woman and a child, continued on to California. This would leave 33 persons in the other party which turned north to Fort Hall, possibly 36 if the Williams' family had three children. Taking the conclusions given above, this would indicate that there were 11 remaining in the missionary party and 22 (or 25) of the Bartleson party who elected to strike for Oregon, bringing the total number of the Bartleson party at the Soda Springs division to 67 (or 70, if the allowance is made for possible Williams' children). It should be noted that in a later recollection,

Bidwell on several occasions used the figure 69. For example, *Echoes,* pp. 22, 37-38.

The interested reader should consult the following work for contrast to the above given view: H. E. Tobie, "From the Missouri to the Columbia, 1841," *Oregon Historical Quarterly,* XXXVIII (1937), 135-159.

Bibliography

MANUSCRIPTS

Bancroft Library, University of California, Berkeley:
John Bidwell, "Early California Reminiscences.' [1877 dictation for H.H. Bancroft.]
Chard & Belden Business Mss.
Joseph B. Chiles, "A Visit to California in Early Times." [1871 dictation for H. H. Bancroft.]
Nicholas Dawson Mss.
Charles Hopper, "Narrative of Charles Hopper a California Pioneer of 1841 written by R. T. Montgomery at Napa 1871." [1871 dictation for H. H. Bancroft.]
Diary of James John. [Microcopy from the original in the Oregon Historical Society Library.]
Diary of James John. [Microcopy from the original in the Rosenbach Foundation, Philadelphia.]
Thomas O. Larkin Papers [unpublished Mss.]
John A. Swan, "Wreck of the Schooner, *Star of the West,* 1845"
Alexander Taylor, *Scrapbook,* No. 7
Mariano Guadalupe Vallejo Papers ["Documents para la Historia de California."]
California Historical Society Library, San Francisco:
Biography and Obituaries [Scrapbooks]
William D. M. Howard Papers
California State Library, Sacramento:
John Bidwell Papers
William Heath Davis Papers
Pierson B. Reading Papers

John A. Sutter Collection

Henry E. Huntington Library, San Marino:
William Heath Davis Papers
Fort Sutter Papers
William Leidesdorff Papers
Dale L. Morgan, [Newspaper Transcripts] *The Mormons and the Far West*
Abel Stearns Papers
Marino Guadalupe Vallejo Papers
Benjamin D. Wilson, "Isaac Graham," James De Barth Shorb Papers [Copy; original in the Bancroft Library.]

Other Repositories:
Josiah Belden Papers, [Private Collection] Clyde Arbuckle, San José
San José City Archives, City Hall

PRINTED DOCUMENTARY SOURCES

Anonymous, "A California Heroine [Recollections of Mrs. Benjamin A. Kelsey]," *The Grizzly Bear Magazine* XVI (February, 1915), 6-7

Anonymous, "California and Oregon," *Colonial Magazine*, V (1841), 229-236.

Ames, Jr., George W., ed., "A Doctor Comes to California. The Diary of John S. Griffin," *California Historical Society Quarterly*, XXI (1942), 193-224, 333-357.

Belden, Josiah, "The First Overland Emigrant Train to New California," *Touring Topics*, 22 (July, 1930), 14-18, 56.

————, "Pastoral California Through Gringo Eyes," *Touring Topics*, 22 (July, 1930), 44-47, 71; (August, 1930), 40-47, 53-54. [The first published, but unedited, version of Belden's 1878 Bancroft dictation.]

Bidwell, John, *A Journey to California, with Observations about the Country, Climate and the Route to this Country* . . . . [Liberty or Weston, Mo.], 184[?]. Under the same title, an edition was published by John H. Nash in San Francisco, 1937.]

————, "Early California Reminiscences [Dictated to O. B. Parkinson of Stockton, California]," *Out West*, XX (January, 1904), 76-78; (February, 1904), 182-188; (March, 1904), 285-287; April,

1904), 377-379; (May, 1904), 467-477; (June, 1904), 559-562; XXI (July, 1904), 79-80; (August, 1904), 193-195. [This version was apparently the one which was republished in C[harles] C. Royce, *John Bidwell: Pioneer, Statesman, Philanthropist* (Chico, California, 1906).]

————, *Echoes of the Past.* Chico *Advertiser*, [n.d.].

————, *Echoes of the Past,* ed. by Milo M. Quaife. Chicago, 1928.

————, *In California Before the Gold Rush.* Introduction by Lindley Bynum. Los Angeles, 1948. [Cited in text as Bidwell, *California.*]

————, "The First Emigrant Train to California," *The American Progress Magazine,* [n.v.] (May, 1910), 5-13. [Reprint of first portion of the article listed immediately below.]

————, "The First Emigrant Train to California," *The Century Illustrated Monthly Magazine,* XLI (November, 1890) 106-130.

————, "Life in California Before the Gold Rush," *The Century Illustrated Monthly Magazine,* XLI (December 1890), 163-183.

————, "Frémont in the Conquest of California," *The Century Illustrated Monthly Magazine,* XLI (February, 1890), 518-525.

Chittenden, Hiram M. and Alfred D. Richardson, eds., *Life, Letters and Travels of Father Pierre-Jean De Smet, S.J., 1801-1872.* 4 vols.; New York, 1905.

[Dawson, Nicholas], *Narrative of Nicholas "Cheyenne" Dawson (Overland to California in '41 & '49, and Texas in '51).* Introduction by Charles L. Camp. San Francisco, 1933.

De Smet, Pierre-Jean, *Letters and Sketches: With a Narrative of a Year's Residence Among the Indian Tribes of the Rocky Mountains,* Philadelphia, 1843.

Dickenson, Luella, *Reminiscences of a Trip Across the Plains in 1846 and Early Days in California.* San Francisco, 1904.

Ewer, John C., ed., *Adventures of Zenas Leonard, Fur Trapper.* Norman, Oklahoma, 1959.

Farquhar, Francis P., ed., *Up and Down California in 1860-1864. The Journal of William H. Brewer* .... Berkeley and Los Angeles, 1949.

Gleason, Duncan, ed. "James Henry Gleason: Pioneer Journal and Letters, 1841-1856," *Historical Society of Southern California Quarterly,* XXXI (1949), 9-52.

Green, Mrs. Edward C., ed., "Journal of Captain John Paty, 1807-

1868," *California Historical Society Quarterly*, XIV (1935), 291-346.

Hammond, George P., ed., *The Larkin Papers.* 7 vols. to date; Berkeley and Los Angeles, 1951-1960.

Hafen, LeRoy R. and Ann W. Hafen, eds., *To the Rockies and Oregon, 1830-1842.* Glendale, California, 1955.

Heath, Minnie B., "Nancy Kelsey—The First Pioneer Woman to Cross [the] Plains," *The Grizzly Bear Magazine*, XL (February, 1937), 3, 7.

Himes, George H., ed., "The Diary of James St. Johns [James John]," St. John [Oregon] *Review*, March 16, 30; April 6, 13, 20, 27, 1906.

New Helvetia Diary. A Record of Events Kept by John A. Sutter and His Clerks . . . . San Francisco, 1939.

Lyman, Chester S., *Around the Horn to the Sandwich Islands and California, 1845-1850.* Edited by Frederick J. Teggart. New Haven, 1924.

Parker, Robert J., Jr., ed., "The Wreck of the *Star of the West*," Historical Society of Southern California *Quarterly*, XXIII (March) 1941), 24-27.

Partoll, Albert J., ed., "Mengarini's Narrative to the Rockies," *Frontier and Midland*, XVIII (1938), 193-202, 258-266. [Reprint, *Sources of Northwest History No. 25* (Missoula, Montana, n.d.).]

Royce, C[harles] C., *John Bidwell: Pioneer, Statesman, Philanthropist.* Chico, California, 1906.

Shuck, Oscar T., comp., *California Scrap-Book: A Repository of Useful Information.* San Francisco, 1869.

Six French Letters[:] Captain John Augustus Sutter to Jean Jacques Vioget, 1842-1843. Sacramento, 1942.

"The California Recollections of Caspar T. Hopkins," *California Historical Society Quarterly*, XXVI (1947), 251-266.

The Diary of Johann August Sutter. San Francisco, 1932.

Thwaites, Reuben G., ed., *Early Western Travels.* 32 vols.; Cleveland, 1904-1907.

Williams, Joseph, *Narrative of a Tour from the State of Indiana to the Oregon Territory in the Years 1841-2.* Cincinnati, 1843.

Woodward, Arthur, ed., "Benjamin David Wilson's Observations on Early Days in California and New Mexico," *Annual Publications* of the Historical Society of Southern California, XVI (1934), 74-150.

SECONDARY SOURCES

Adams, Ephraim D., "British Interests in California," *American Historical Review*, XIV (1909), 744-763.

Arbuckle, Clyde, "Grove C. Cook," *Westways*, 43 (December, 1951), 19.

Argonauts of California. New York, 1890.

Artistic Homes of California. San Francisco, 1887-1888.

Bailey, Paul, *Sam Brannan and the California Mormons*. Los Angeles, 1953.

Bancroft, Hubert H., *History of California*. 7 vols.; San Francisco, 1886-1890.

Barrows, H. D., "Don David W. Alexander," *Annual Publications* of the Historical Society of Southern California, IV (1897), 43-45.

Benjamin, Marcus, *John Bidwell, Pioneer. A Sketch of His Career*. Washington, 1907.

Carosso, Vincent P., *The California Wine Industry, 1830-1896*. Berkeley and Los Angeles, 1951.

Caughey, John W., *California*. Rev. ed.; Englecliff, New Jersey, 1959.

Cleland, Robert G., *A History of California: The American Period*. New York, 1922.

————, *From Wilderness to Empire*. New York, 1944.

Dakin, Susanna B., *The Lives of William Hartnell*. Stanford, California, 1949.

Englehardt, Fr. Zephrin [Charles A.], *The Missions and Missionaries of California*. 4 vols.; San Francisco, 1908-1915.

Farnham, Thomas J., *The Early Days of California*. Philadelphia, 1852.

————, *Travels in the Great Western Prairies*. Poughkeepsie, New York, 1841.

Foote, H[orace] S., ed., *Pen Pictures from the Garden of the World, or Santa Clara County, California*. Chicago, 1888.

Hafen, LeRoy R., "Fraeb's Last Fight and How Battle Creek Got Its Name." *Colorado Magazine*, VII (1930), 97-101.

————, and W[illiam] H. Ghent, *Broken Hand, The Life of Thomas Fitzpatrick*. Denver, 1931.

Hall, Frederic, *The History of San José and Surroundings, With Biographical Sketches of Early Settlers.* San Francisco, 1871.

Hawgood, John A., "John C. Frémont and the Bear Flag Revolution," *University of Birmingham* [England] *Historical Journal,* VII (1959), 80-100.

Hill, Joseph J., "Antoine Robidoux, Kingpin in the Colorado River Fur Trade, 1824-1844." *Colorado Magazine,* VII (1930), 125-132.

Hunt, Rockwell D., *John Bidwell, Prince of California Pioneers.* Caldwell, Idaho, 1942.

Hussey, John A., "New Light Upon Talbot H. Green," *California Historical Society Quarterly,* XVIII (1939), 32-63.

Johnson, Allen and Dumas Malone, eds., *Dictionary of American Biography.* 20 vols.; New York, 1920-1937.

Lyman, George D., *John Marsh, Pioneer.* New York, 1930.

Mason, Paul, "Constitutional History of California," *Constitution of the State of California . . . 1957.* Sacramento, [1957], pp. 243-254.

McDermott, John F., "De Smet's Illustrator: Father Nicholas Point," *Nebraska History,* XXXIII (1952), 35-40.

McKittrick, Myrtle M., *Vallejo, Son of California.* Portland, Oregon, 1944.

Menefee, C[ampbell] A., *Historical and Descriptive Sketch Book of Napa, Sonoma, Lake and Mendocino . . . .* Napa City, California, 1873.

Miller, David E., "The First Wagon Train to Cross Utah, 1841," *Utah Historical Quarterly,* XXX (Winter, 1962), 41-51.

Morgan, Dale L., *Jedediah Smith and the Opening of the West.* Indianapolis and New York, 1953.

Mumey, Nolie, *The life of Jim Baker.* Denver, 1931

Munro-Fraser, J. P., *History of Santa Clara County.* San Francisco, 1881.

Nunis, Jr., Doyce B., *Andrew Sublette, Rocky Mountain Prince, 1808-1853.* Los Angeles, 1960.

————, "The Enigma of the Sublette Overland Party, 1845." *Pacific Historical Review,* XXVIII (1959), 331-349.

Ogden, Adele, "Boston Hide Droghers Along California Shores," *California Historical Society Quarterly,* VIII (1929), 289-305.

Phelps, Alonzo, *Contemporary Biography of California's Representative Men.* 2 vols.; San Francisco, 1881-1882.

Rolle, Andrew, *An American in California: The Biography of William Heath Davis, 1822-1909.* San Marino, California, 1956.

Shuck, Oscar T., *Sketches of Leading and Representative Men of San Francisco.* San Francisco, 1875.

Sommervogel, Carlos, ed., *Biblioteque de la Compagnie de Jesus.* 11 vols.; Brussels and Paris, 1890-1919.

Soulé, Frank, *et al., The Annals of San Francisco.* New York, 1854.

Tobie, H. E., "From the Missouri to the Columbia, 1841," *Oregon Historical Quarterly*, XXXVIII (1937), 135-159.

Underhill, Reuben L., *From Cowhide to Golden Fleece.* Stanford, California, 1939.

Wagner, Henry, R., *The Plains and the Rockies.* Revised by Charles L. Camp. 3rd ed.; Columbus, Ohio, 1953.

Wallace, William S., *Antoine Robidoux.* Los Angeles, 1953.

Zollinger, James P., *Sutter, The Man and His Empire.* New York and London, 1939.

NEWSPAPERS

Alta California, February 8, 1849; February 1, 1852; March 23, April 15, 1866.

Blue Lake *Advocate*, June 13, 20, 1957.

Californian, February 16, 1848.

Daily Missouri Republican, September 28, 1841.

Monterey *Cypress*, May 25, 1889.

Napa County *Reporter*, March 23, 1872.

Napa *Register*, March 16, 1872.

New York *Tribune*, April 25, 1892.

Niles Register, August 15, 1840; May 22, September 11, October 16, 1841; January 28, February 11, 1843.

Sacramento *Daily Democratic State Journal*, October 27, 1855.

Sacramento *Union*, April 25, 1892.

San Francisco *Call*, April 24, June 19, 1892.

San Francisco *Chronicle*, June 12, 1856; December 3, 1904.

San Francisco *Examiner*, June 3, 1869; February 5, 1893.

San Francisco *Evening Bulletin*, July 27, 1868.

San Francisco *Herald*, June 15, 1856.

San José *Mercury Herald*, June 17, 1934.

San José *Tribune*, July 23, 1856.

Index

Paul.

Griffin, Dr. John S., 112, *n. 95.*

Gwin, William M., 108, *n. 74.*

Gwinn, Frank, 106, *n. 62.*

Gutierrez, Nicholas, 100, *n. 33.*

Hampton, Wade, 67.

Hartnell, William, 67; 105, *n. 61.*

Hastings, Lansford W., 106. *n. 65.*

Hayes, Rutherford B., 20.

Heath, Minnie B., 22.

Henshaw, George, 37; 127.

Hensley, Samuel J., 67; 106, *n. 65.*

Higuera, Joaquin, 45; 99, *n. 25.*

Hill, David F., 127.

Hixley, see Hensley, Samuel J.

Hopper, Charles, 16; 20; 37; 97, *n. 17;* 102, *n. 46;* 127; 128.

Howard, William D.M., 17; 31, *n. 26;* 112, *n. 97.*

Howard & Mellus, 76.

Huber, Henry, 37; 127.

Huet, Charles, 126.

Iddings, Mrs. Lewis Morris, 32, *n. 34.*

Ide, William B., 69; 107, *n. 68.*

Independence Rock, 14; 38.

Irving, Washington, 15.

John, James, 23; 26; 37; 98, *n. 24;* 127; 131; 134.

Johnstone, Andrew, 101, *n. 40.*

Jones, ———, 128; 130; 131; 132; 134.

Jones, J.M., 131; 132.

Jones, John C., 113, *n. 99.*

Jones, Sarah Margaret, 111, *n. 90;* 112, *n. 91.*

Jones, Thomas, 37; 97, *n. 21;* 127; 131.

Jones, Com. Thomas Ap Catesby, 62.

Jones, Zachariah, 111, *n. 90.*

Kansas River, 37.

Kearney, Stephen W., 71; 81.

Kelsey, Andrew, 37; 97, *n. 21;* 127.

Kelsey, Benjamin, 37; 97, *n. 16;* 127.

Kelsey, Isaac, 95, *n. 10;* 128, 133.

Kelsey, Josiah, see Kelsey, Isaac.

Kelsey, Nancy A. (Mrs. Benjamin), 22; 37; 95, *n. 10;* 127; 133.

Kelsey, Rebecca, 114, *n. 100.*

Kelsey, Mrs. Samuel, 95, *n. 10;* 132; 133.

Kelsey, Samuel, 128; 133.

Kern, Edward M., 114, *n. 102.*

Knight, William, 67.

Knight's Ferry, California, 44.

La Mesa, Battle of, 81.

Larkin, Thomas O., 17; 18; 58; 62; 64; 66; 89; 90; 100, *n. 34;* 101, *n. 40, 41, 42, 43;* 102, *n. 47;* 103, *n. 50, 51;* 104, *n. 57;* 105, *n. 60;* 113, *n. 97;* 114, *n. 101;* 117; 118; 119; 121; 122; 125.

Lee, Daniel, 9.

Lee, Jason, 9.

Leese, Jacob P., 80; 98, *n. 24,*

*This book has been designed and printed
at The Talisman Press, Georgetown, California,
in an edition limited to 750 copies.
November, 1962.*